LENNY KRAVITZ

FLASH

teNeues

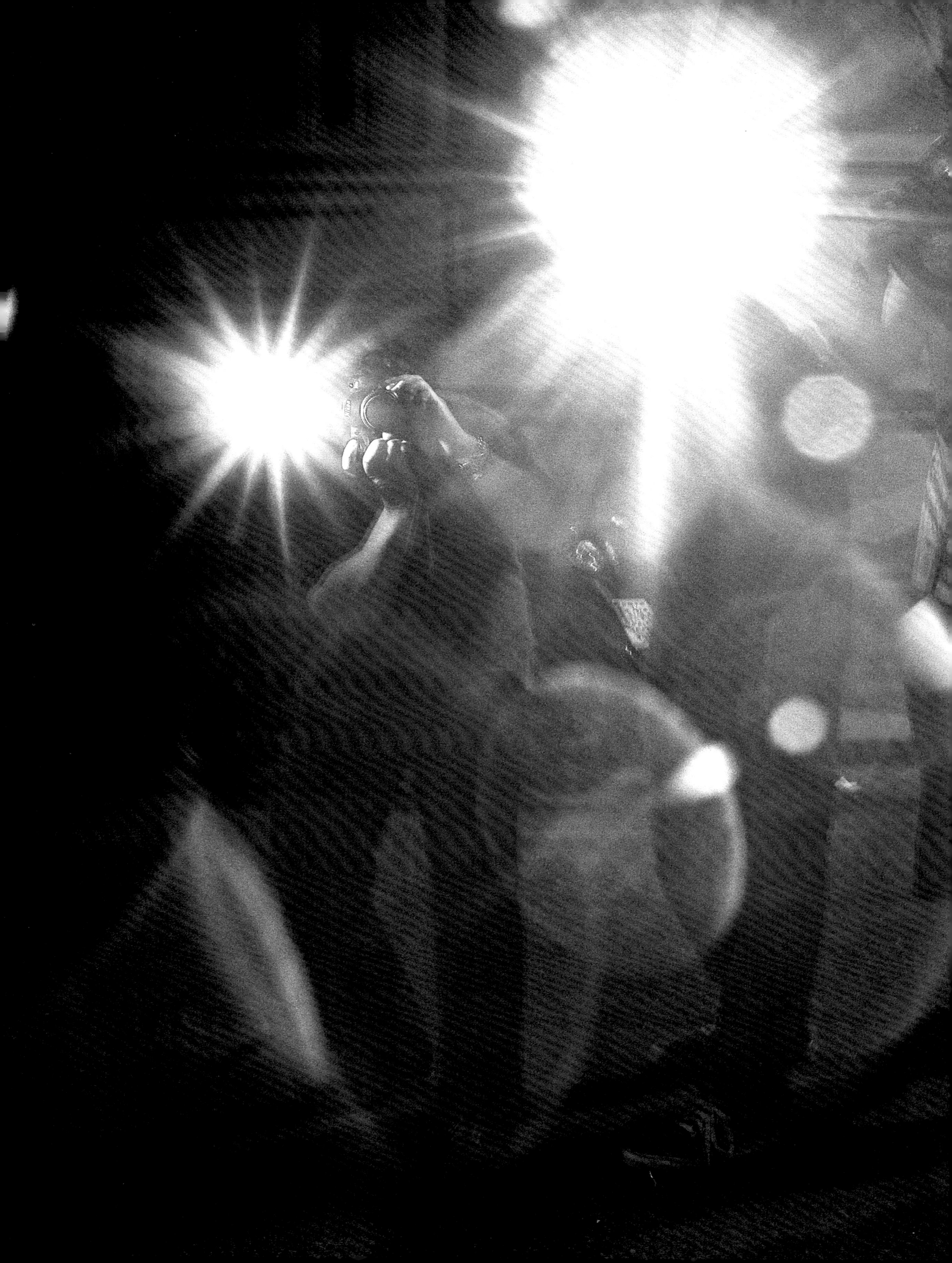

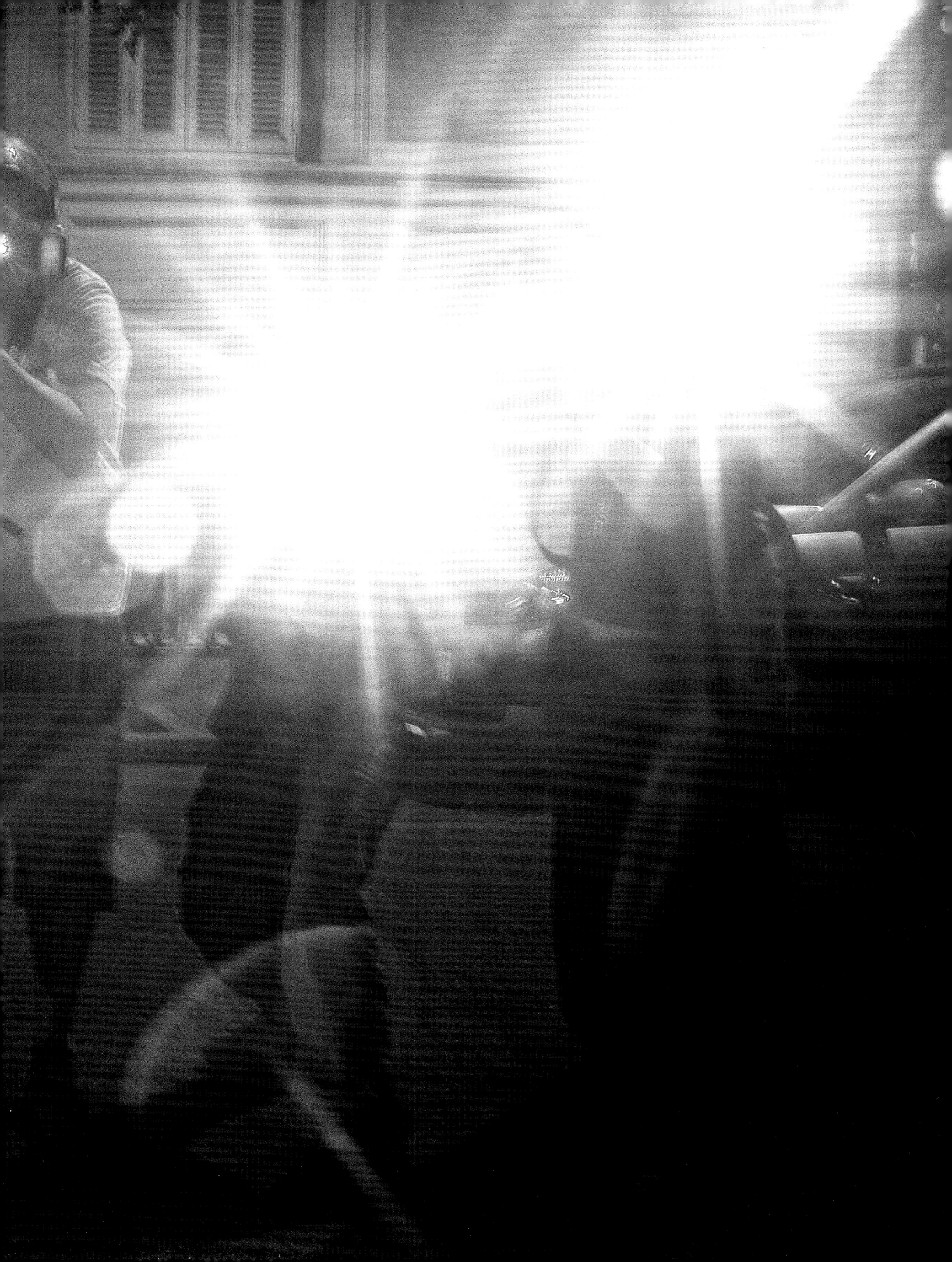

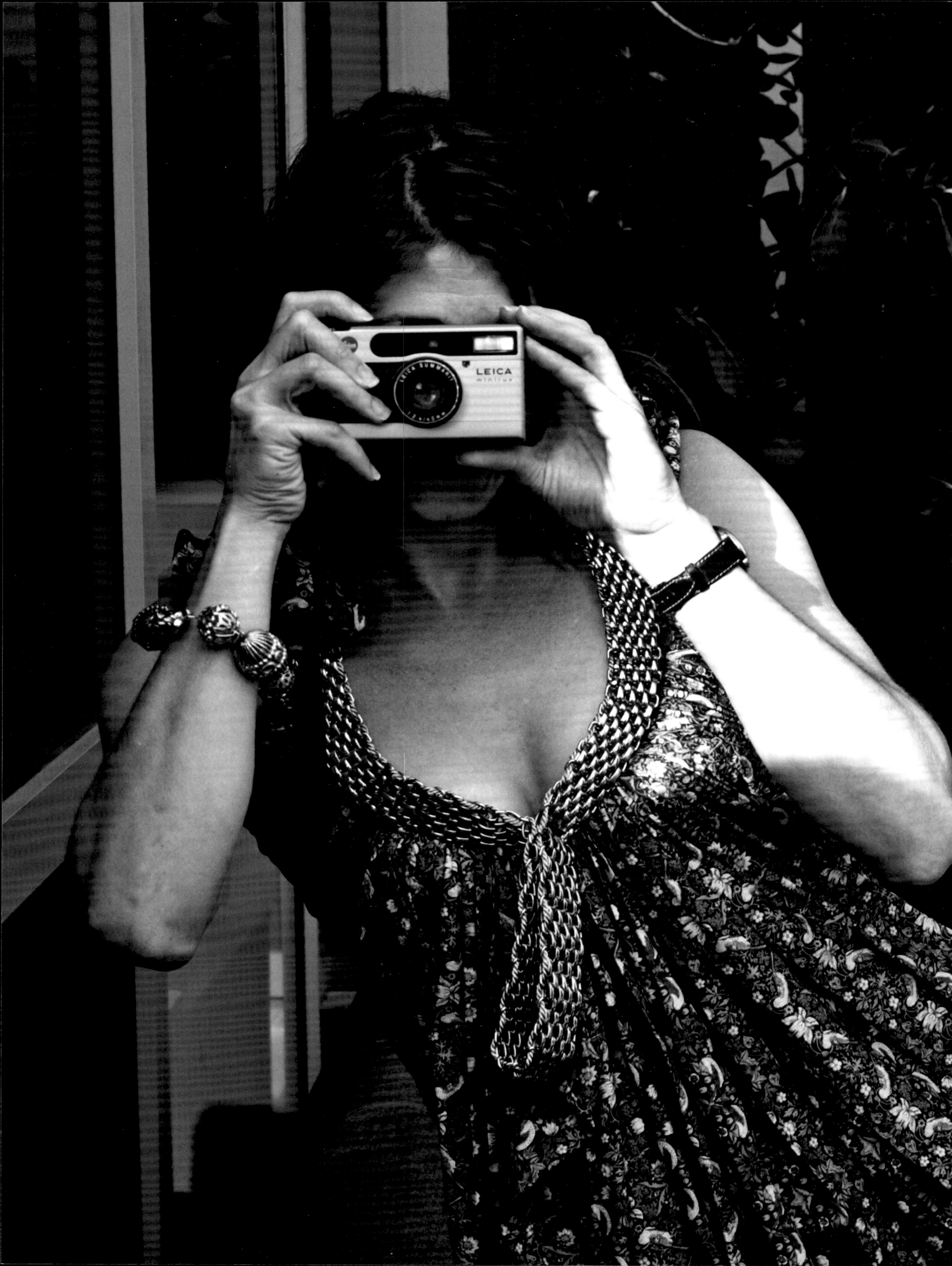
LEICA

INTRODUCTION

It's interesting that the very people who chase me to take my photographs have become the subjects of my first photo exhibition and book.

Through turning the lens back on them, I have indirectly taken a deeper look at myself and the surreal world that I live in when on the road.

What once was intrusive has now become a beautiful moment of a dance between the hunter and it's prey.

Lenny Kravitz and Jean-Baptiste Mondino met twenty-five years ago, when Mondino signed on to direct the video for the song "Be" from Kravitz's debut album *Let Love Rule*. That began a friendship that continues to this day. As a photographer and video director, Mondino has worked with artists such as Prince, Madonna, Serge Gainsbourg, Vanessa Paradis, and David Bowie. Beyond his iconic status as a musician, Kravitz has distinguished himself as both a designer and an actor. Now, with *FLASH*, he has published his first book of photographs. In this conversation, Kravitz and Mondino discuss *FLASH*, the value of instinct, and life in front of and behind the camera. – Anthony DeCurtis

Lenny Kravitz: It's funny, Jean-Baptiste, I've never had a serious conversation with you in my life, so this should be interesting. [laughter] But first of all, I should say that this book wouldn't even exist if it weren't for you. I've always had an interest in photography. I find it to be quite magical, the capturing of a moment. And after I purchased a Leica and decided to go out and shoot, I showed you these photographs. When you saw them you said that this should be the first work of mine that people see. I wasn't thinking about anything like that, but you said that I should do something with them because nothing like them had been seen. So you put the thought in my mind, and I'm quite thankful for that.

JBM: First of all, when you started taking pictures, you started by shooting beautiful girls. [laughter] Beautiful photography of women, which makes sense. But suddenly I saw that you had not one or two, but ten or fifteen or twenty pictures that were amazing in terms of the beauty of the image itself. It wasn't just the concept. At the same time, there was your point of view of being someone that people take pictures of all the time, of your being a pop star and being chased by people, and you yourself taking pictures of them. That's why I call these photos flashback pictures. Your point of view is amazing because these pictures introduce us to your world, to what you're thinking.

When you're surrounded by photographers who are yelling at you, it can be exciting, but it's chaotic and you can feel like you're trapped. But you manage a kind of detachment, looking at them with kindness. There's no fear. To be capable of that, to be able to take a picture back at the people who are trying to take pictures of you, it's unbelievable. Showing us what you see, what you're facing. The point of view is brilliant, and the quality can't be denied. You're walking in the middle of a nightmare, and you can take a picture of it and frame it well. It's amazing.

LK: Yeah, some of the situations are a little chaotic. Like there's one picture of me inside a store, where you see all the people pressed against the window and I'm inside where they have these leather coats and leather bags. I mean, I got chased into that place. It ended up being a really wonderful photograph,

CONVERSATION

but I was literally running down the street. And once I got inside the store, and I saw the people pressed against the window like that and they weren't leaving, I figured, "Okay, well, here I go. I'm going to shoot that."

I mean, this whole project happened by accident. I got my Leica so that I could walk around when I have days off on tour and take photographs and just see what happens. And that's what I did. And everywhere I went, I got bombarded. So one day I just decided that I was fed up with being bothered, and I figured, well, let me turn this into something. I came here to shoot photographs, but now I can't, because there's people all around me. So let me just shoot them. And that's how it began. It was really like that. I had no intention of ever doing anything like this. It was just a byproduct of what my life is like while I'm trying to walk down the street.

JBM: That's another interesting thing about this book. It's really something that could have been done by Andy Warhol, because it's a different point of view. It's the scary point of view of the pop culture that we've created. On the one hand we love it, and on the other hand, it's a little frightening. There's nothing between you and the crowd.

LK: And it's hard to move back from the crowd because I chose to use a manual camera. I could have had an automatic and just pop the picture and run. But I'm surrounded by these people, and I have to read my light and I have to focus, and I'm trying to run and move at the same time. So it becomes quite an exercise.

JBM: It's like when WeeGee would be in the middle of a crime scene or something, but he would still be very cool-headed. There's something very calm about these pictures, even in the middle of all the ruckus. That's what I find incredibly interesting. And when I saw the final project, I realized that it was even stronger than I thought.

The pictures you take are calm, you know? I find it incredibly moving, and I don't know where you get that from. Maybe because you're half black, half Jewish, half feminine, half a pop star, a great cook, a great designer, a good actor, a great friend. [laughter] And you don't age. It's true! Can you imagine? The list is too long. It's almost embarrassing, you know?

LK: Oh, man, you talk all this nonsense, but you have it all. I mean, everything. You play it down and are very modest, but the wonderful thing about you is that you do not look back. You're always looking forward. And I understand that quality. I do the same thing. What I've done, I've done, and I don't want to do it anymore. I'm on to the next thing. I'm always trying to be better, to grow, and to reach a new plateau. But you're such a visionary.

JBM: For me, you know, I like photography, but I never wanted to be a photographer. It just happened. I wanted to be a guitarist. But I had the problem of not having the right hair, because you cannot be bald and play guitar. [laughter] There is not one famous guitarist with a bald head, so I knew in this life I had to do something else.

So I started doing record covers for friends, people I knew. What I love about photography though is that I like to serve my subjects. I become the person I shoot. So some days I'm a girl, sometimes I'm black, sometimes I'm gay, you know what I'm saying? That's the beauty of it for me.

LK: I love using different media to express myself. Photography is something I was always interested in from when I was a child, when I saw my father's camera. He had an old Leica that he had in Vietnam.

JBM: For me, I started to become a photographer when the Polaroid came out, because I didn't know how to load a camera. Actually I didn't have a camera. I still don't have one, because I don't take pictures in real life. But I'm surrounded by people who are obsessed with photography, and they're obsessed with technique. Actually, technique is not very important once you just learn the technique you need for what you want to do. In this book, for instance, it's the point of view that matters, and the technique follows from that.

LK: Whether it's music, photography, or design, I work on feeling. I mean, I didn't go to school for design. I didn't go to school for photography. I learn the basic techniques along the way—if you want to get the image, the light has to be right and you have to focus. But as far as composition, that's just my eye. It's my point of view.

JBM: One thing I've found about taking pictures that I cannot explain is that what you're thinking as you take the picture prints into the photograph. If you are scared, your pictures look scared. If you are loving, your pictures will be loving. If you desire somebody sexually, you can tell in the picture. I don't know what it is. And that's what I like in your pictures: you are fearless, so there is no fear. Without trying to be arty, there is just a very uncomplicated sense of looking at these people and saying, "Look at this." It's like some kind of Fellini movie. You find the beauty in it. It's almost as if you were a woman, because it's not a male point of view. There's a real gentleness to it.

CONVERSATION

LK: I find beauty in everything. When I say beauty, I don't mean that it's clichéd beautiful, but some kind of form, composition, something that aesthetically pleases me. So when I'm out and I see these situations, there's something inside me, my eye, that says, "Wow, that's beautiful," or "Look at this guy's face," or "Look at this woman." It's instinctual. When I feel it, I shoot it.

JBM: But when you do, it's probably very noisy, with people yelling and moving around. What I find interesting is how at that moment you forget about the role you have as somebody desired, somebody these people want to photograph, and you become a spectator. You look at it as if you were completely out of the picture. It's the same thing I capture in you when you're coming off stage, and you instantly come back to life.

I really admire that after I see you on stage singing, facing thousands of people yelling and screaming, when you walk off stage, you get right back to the real world. You're back with us. Most artists need time to adapt themselves to reality. But you have the capacity of adjusting right away. I never saw that in any other musician I know.

LK: I crave what we call "real life." But, for me, it's all real. When I'm on stage, I'm not a different person, it's just a more extroverted part of me. But what I crave is intimacy with friends and family and loved ones, so when I come off stage and I see you or a cousin or a god-daughter or a sister or an aunt or a friend, that's what feeds me, so I immediately pop right back into "real life" because that's ultimately what I desire.

JBM: In a strangely beautiful way, I think this is the best self-portrait book that I've ever seen. Because it is a self-portrait. From the inside. So once again, Lenny, you've made a hit, which makes sense, because you're used to it.

LK: Obviously, we're friends. We joke around a lot. We've spent a lot of years together. We've vacationed together. We have a lot of mutual friends and family. And we're family. I've seen your kids grow up. You've seen my kid grow up. But you're such an amazing artist that I respect so much, and being around you over the years has taught me a lot and inspired me a great deal.

How fortunate am I to meet people like you who come into my life to work with me and do photography and videos and bring all of your wonderful magic to my music? How wonderful it is that I get to watch you and learn from you? That's such a blessed place to be. It's a wonderful gift.

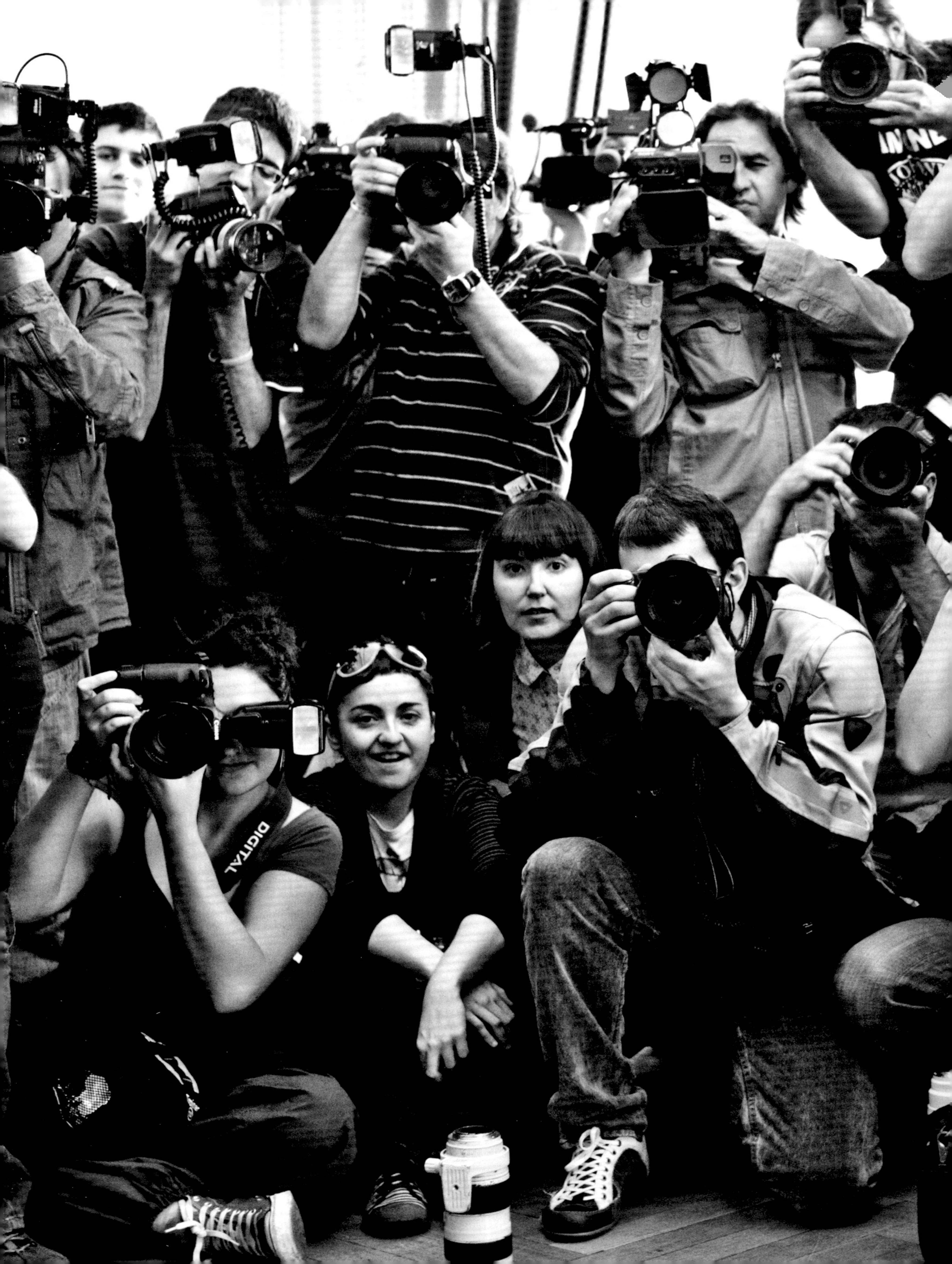
DIGITAL

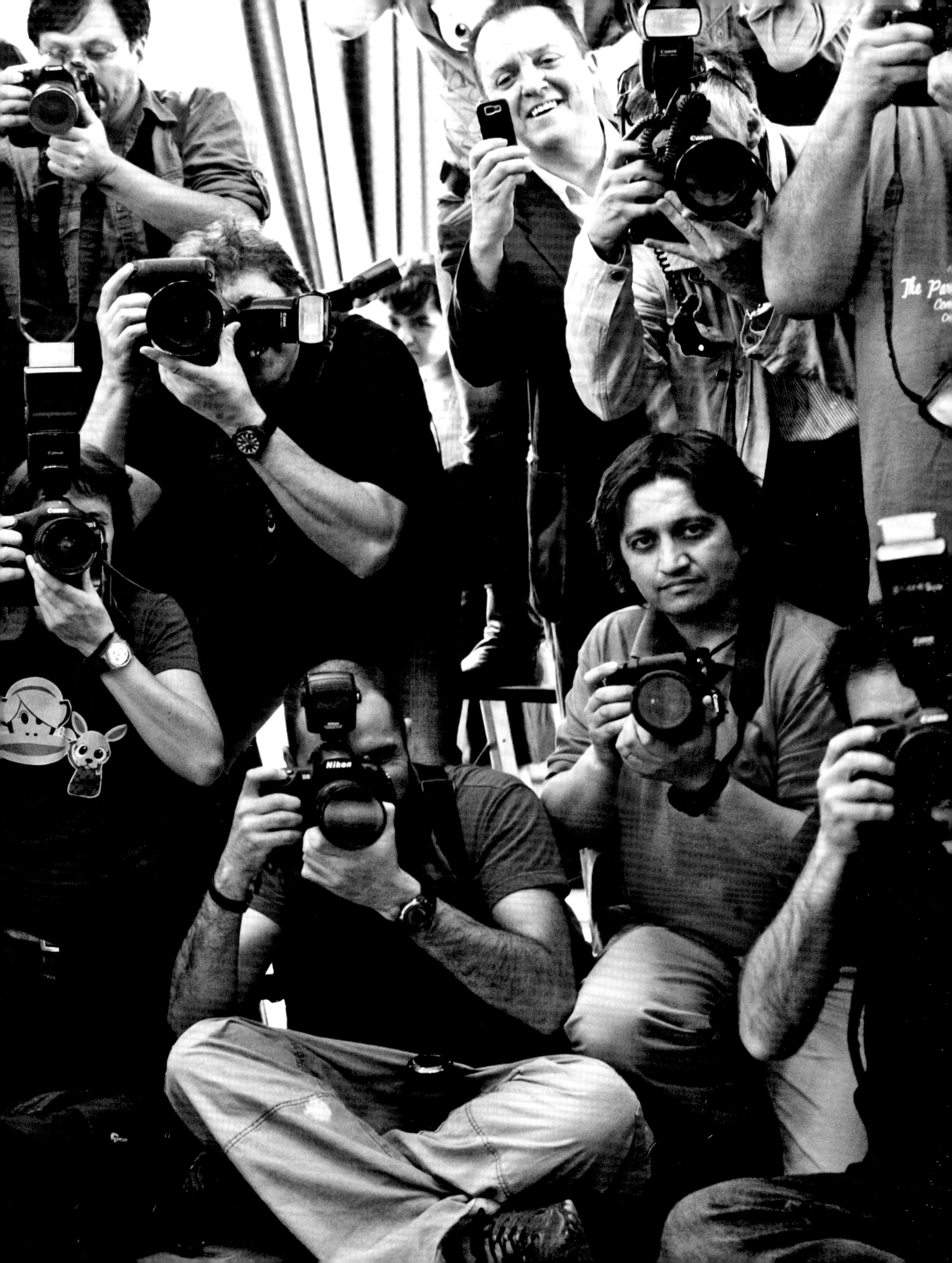
Canon
Nikon

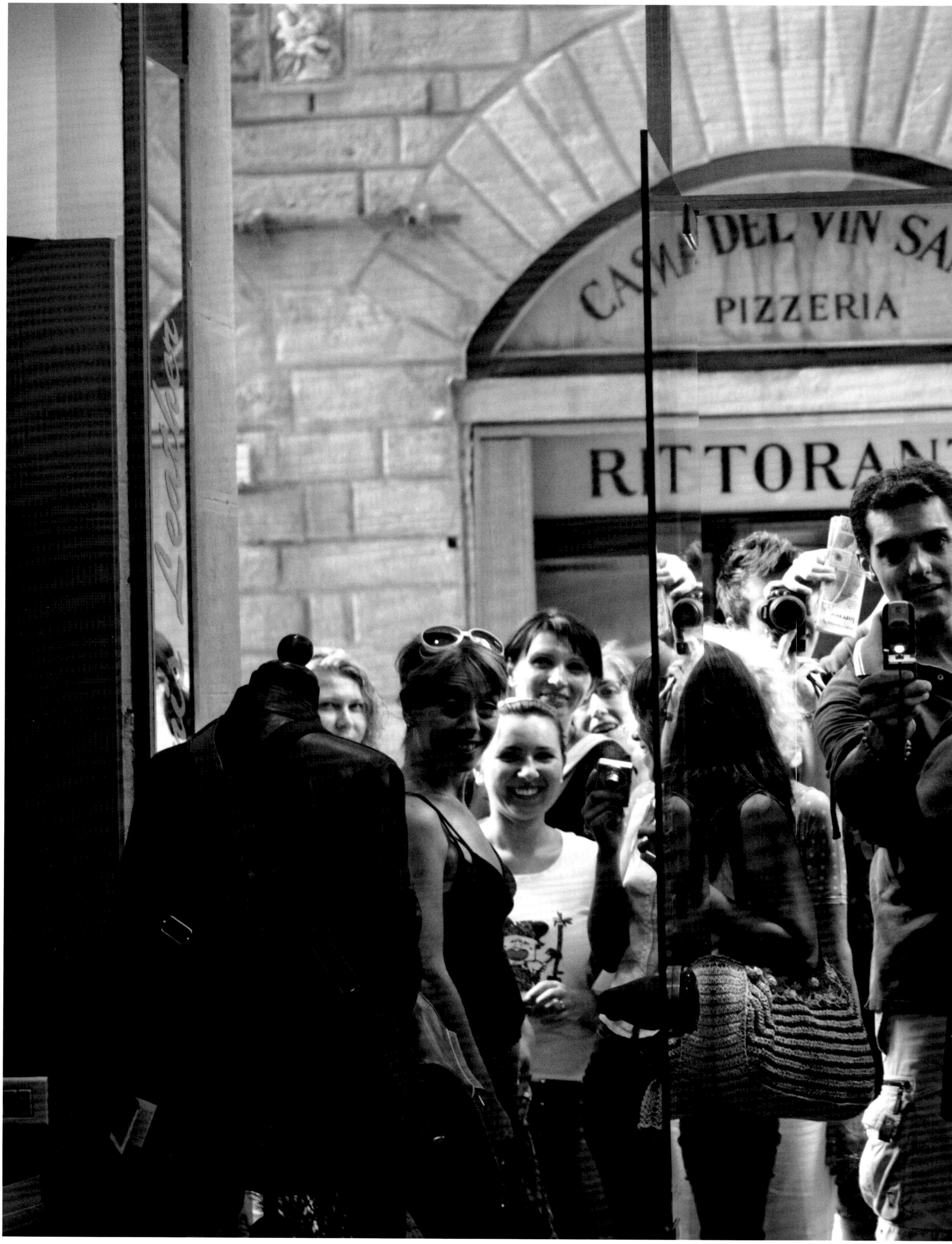
DEL VIN
PIZZERIA

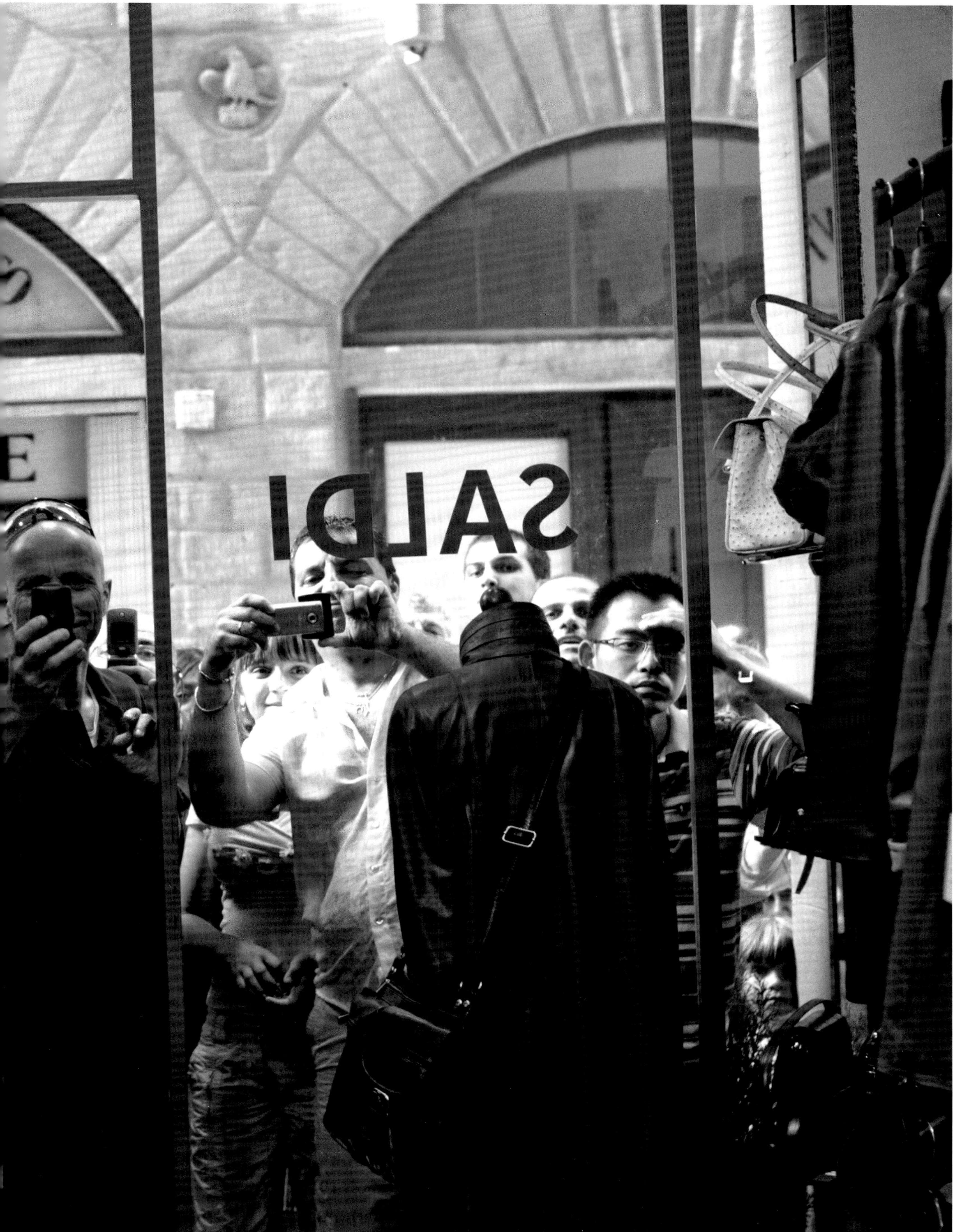
SALDI

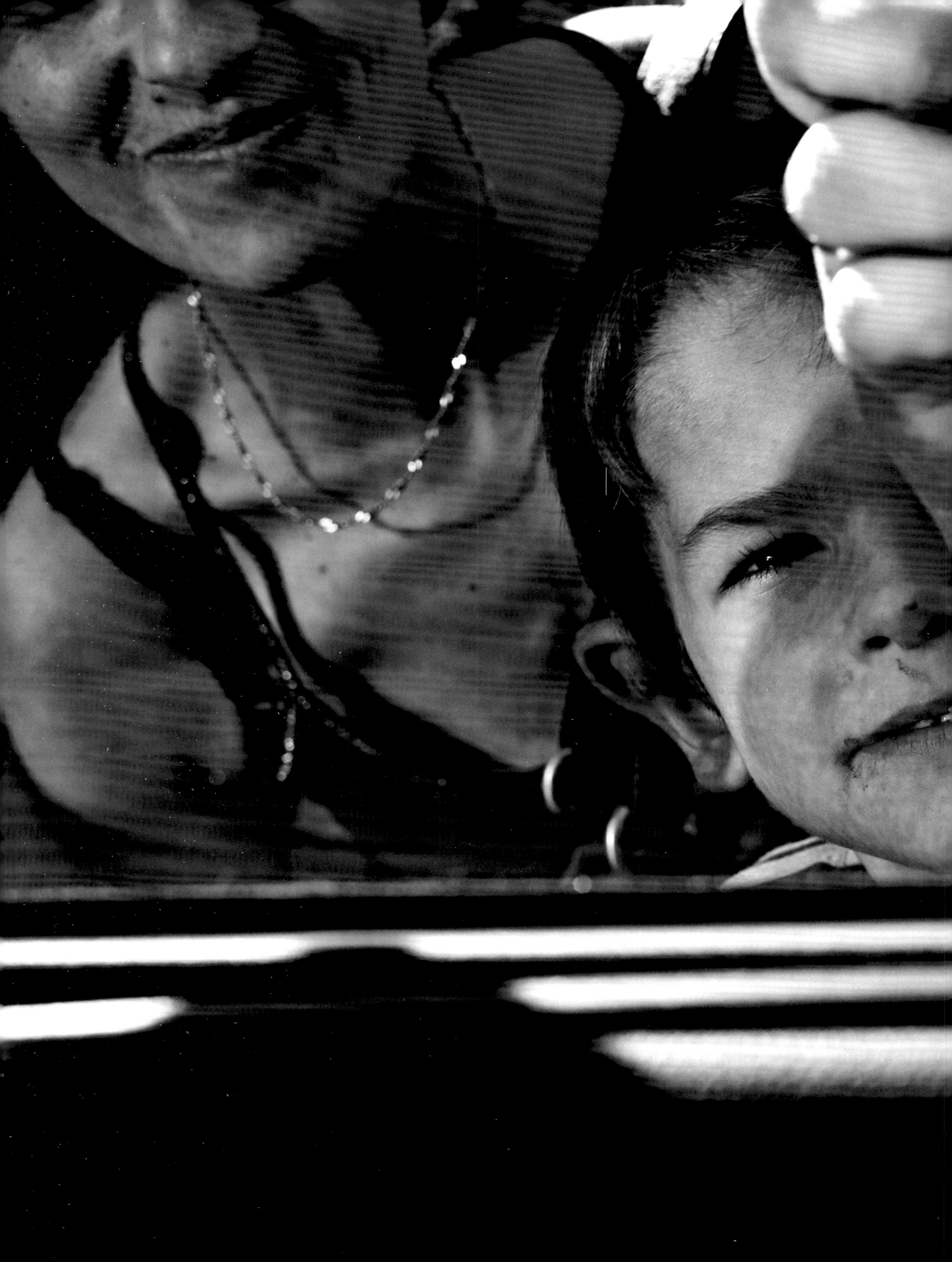

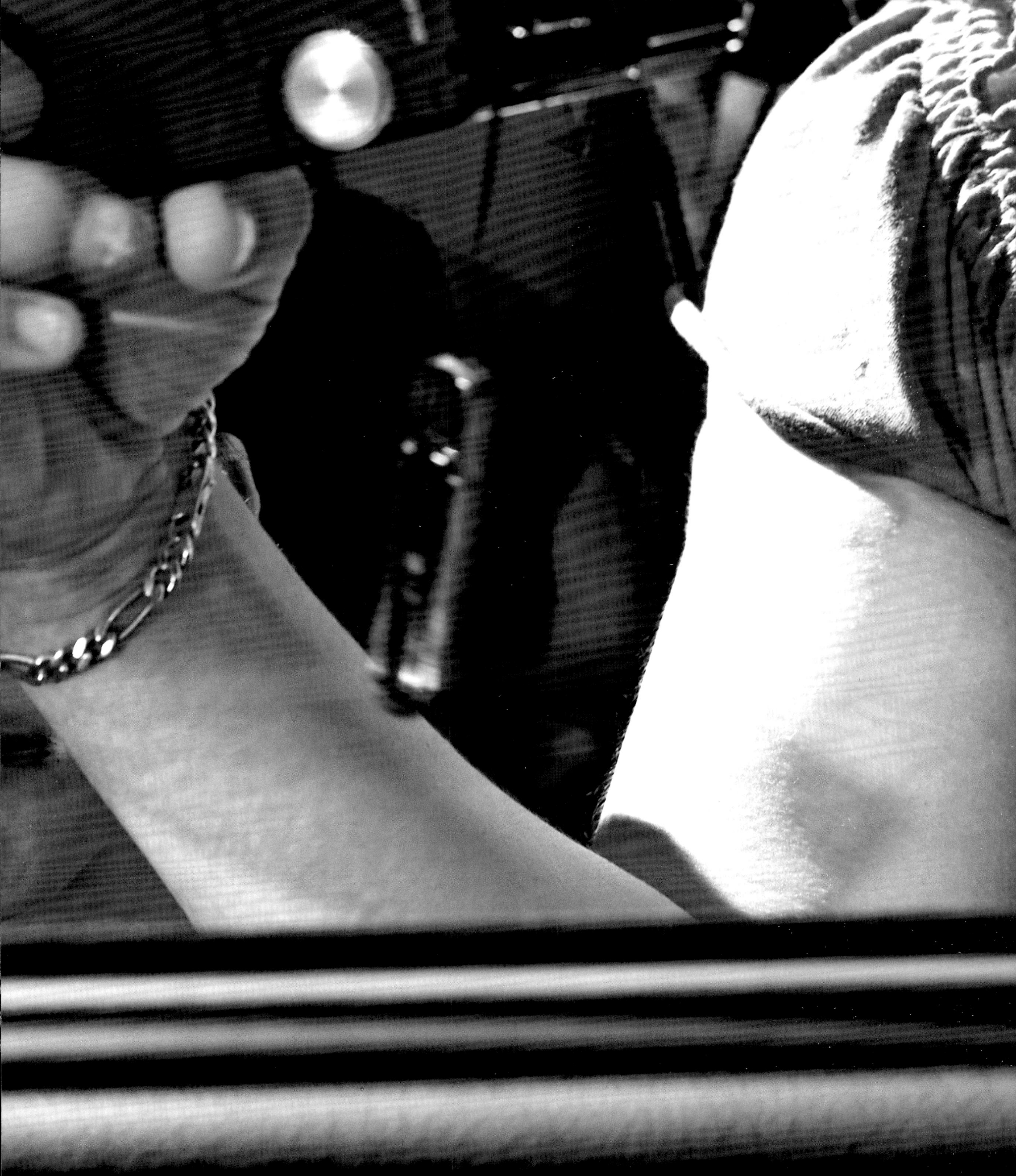

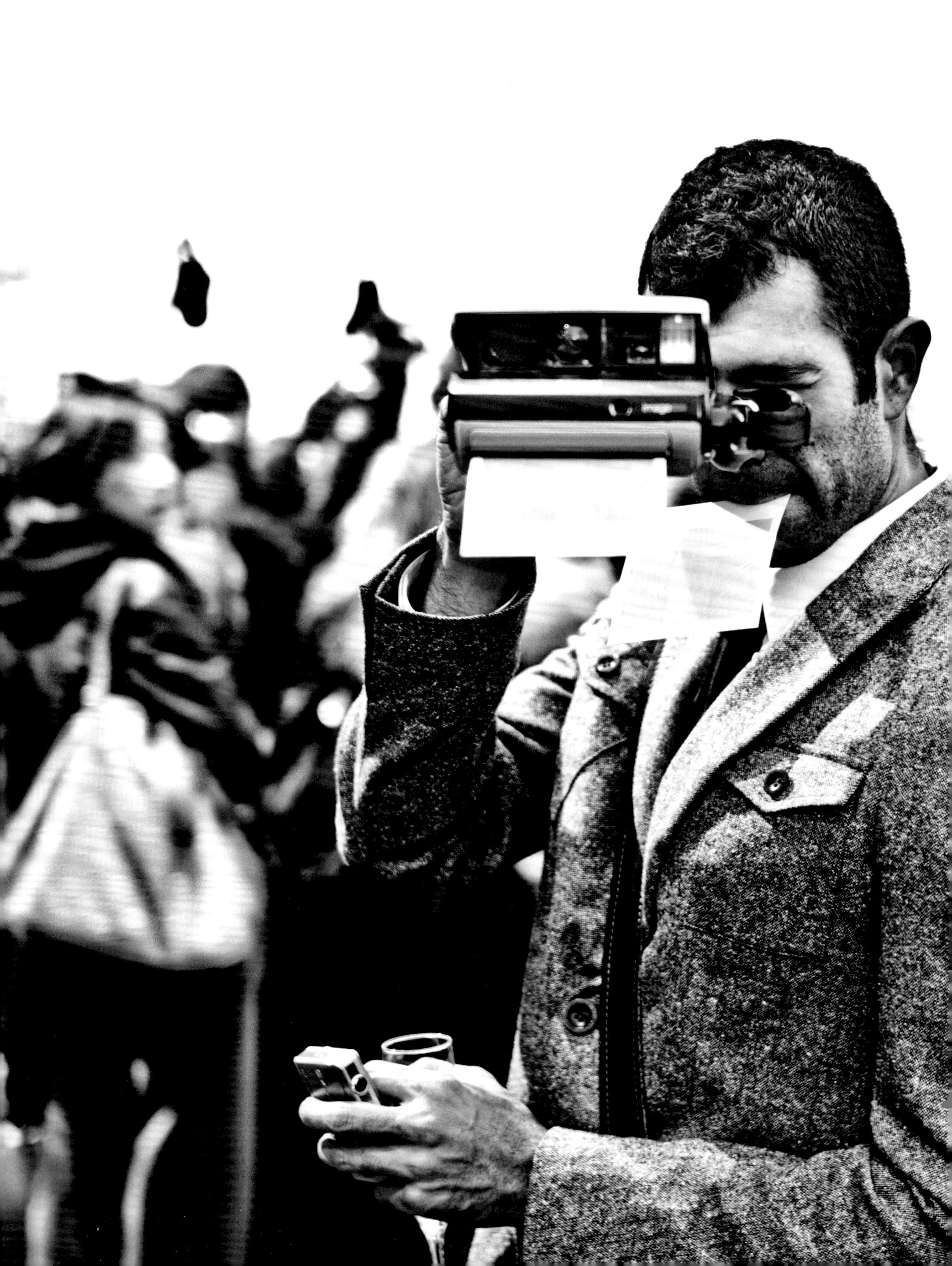

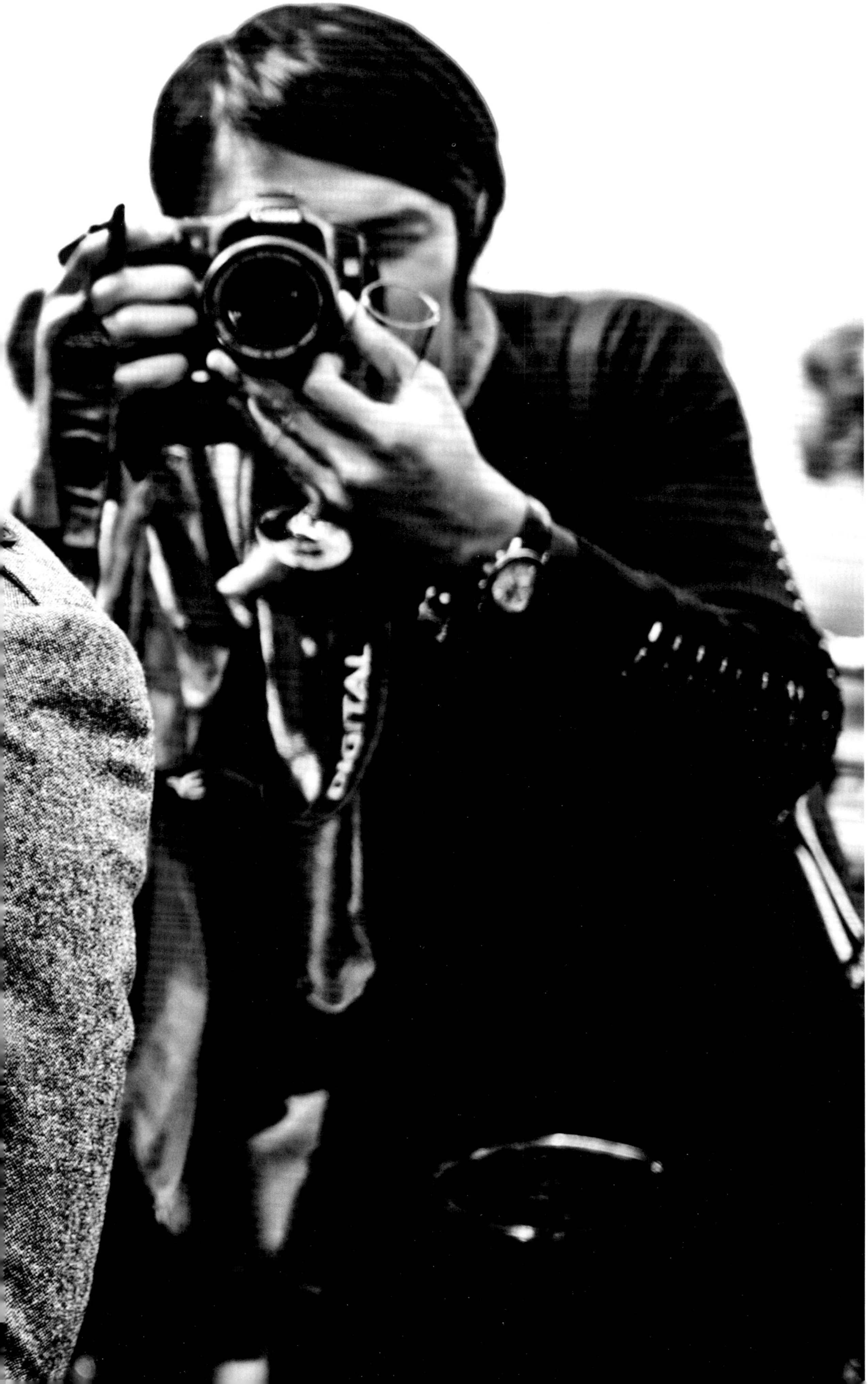
DIGITAL

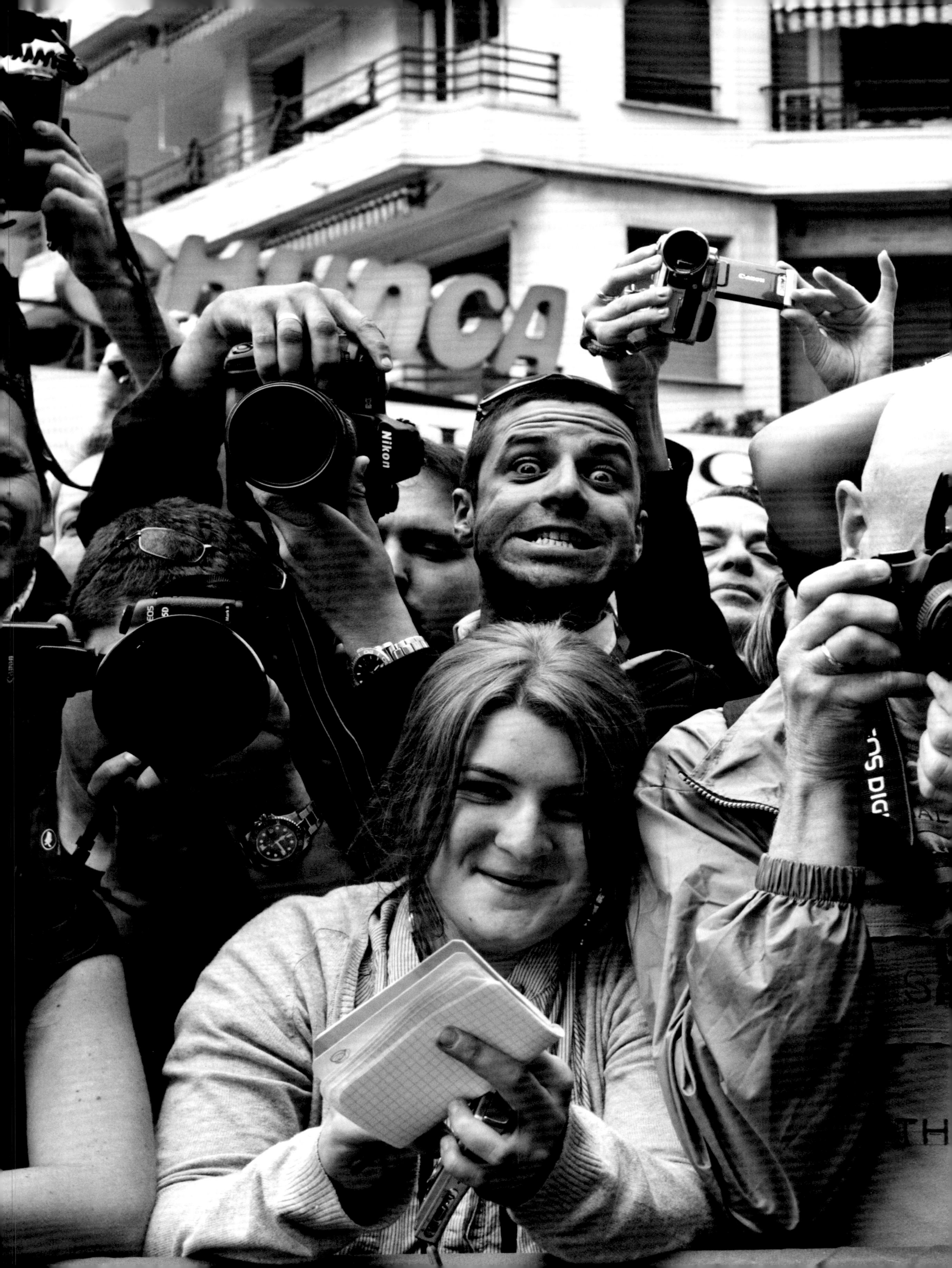
Nikon

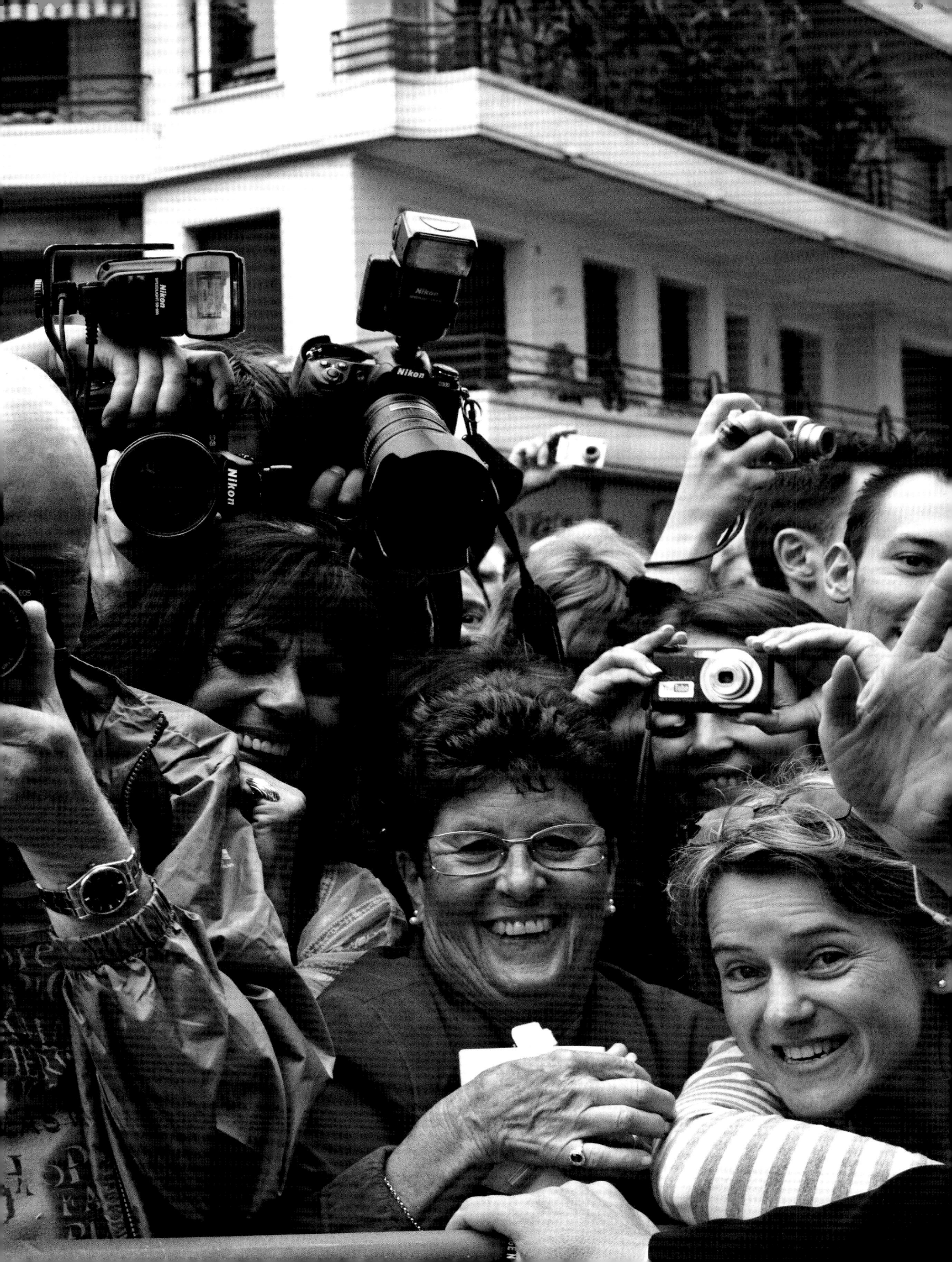
Nikon
Nikon
Nikon
Nikon

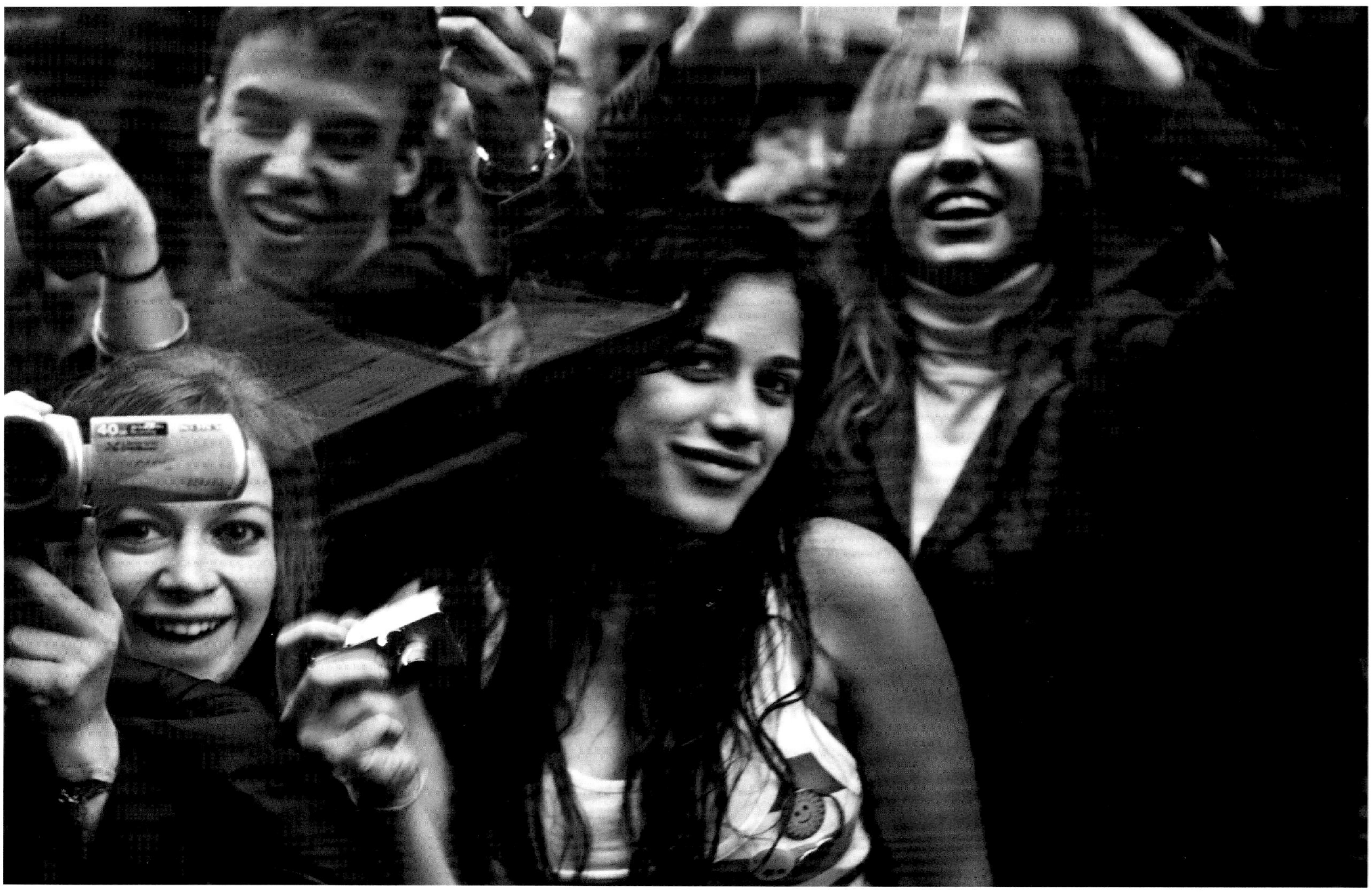

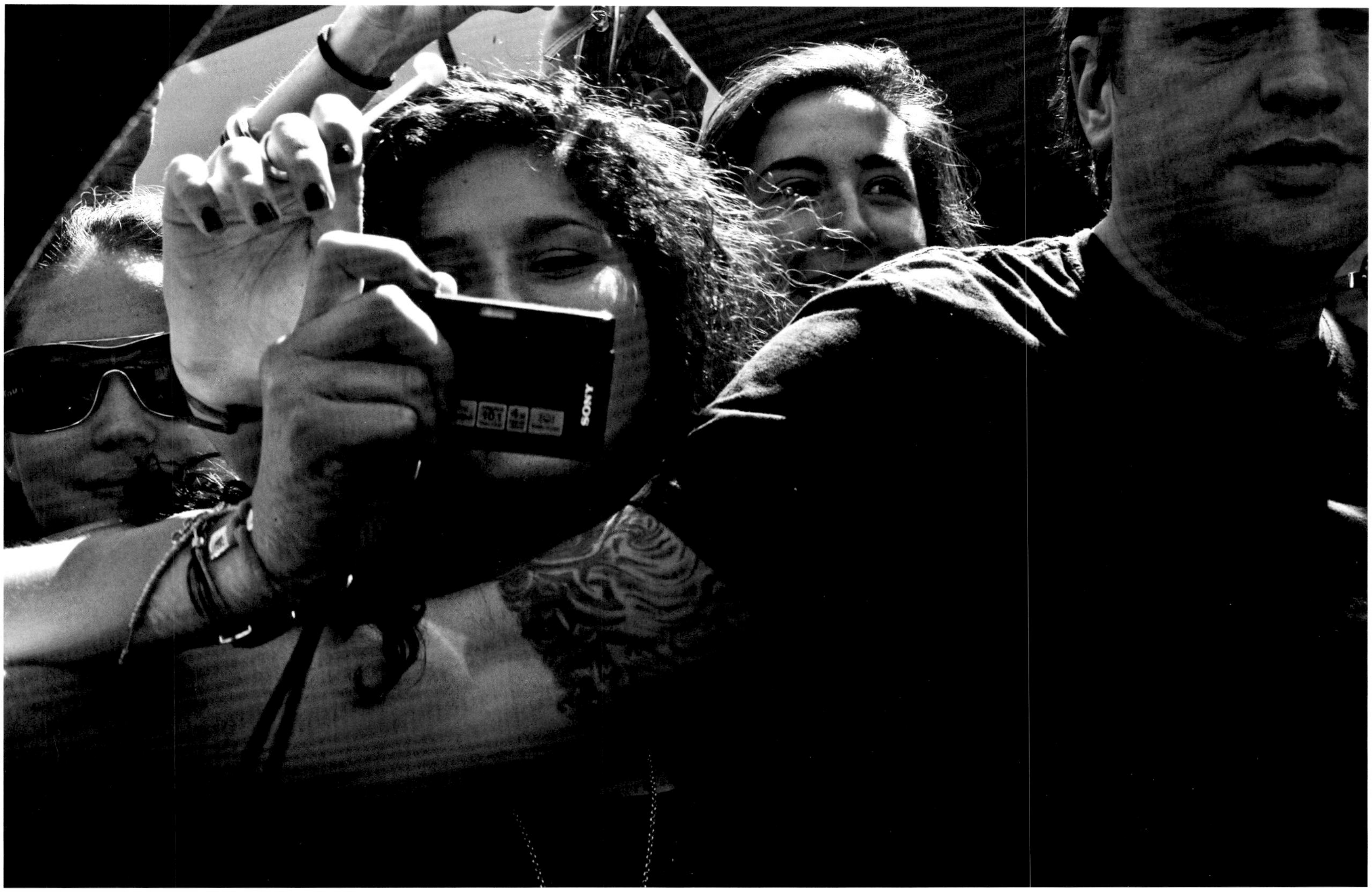
SONY

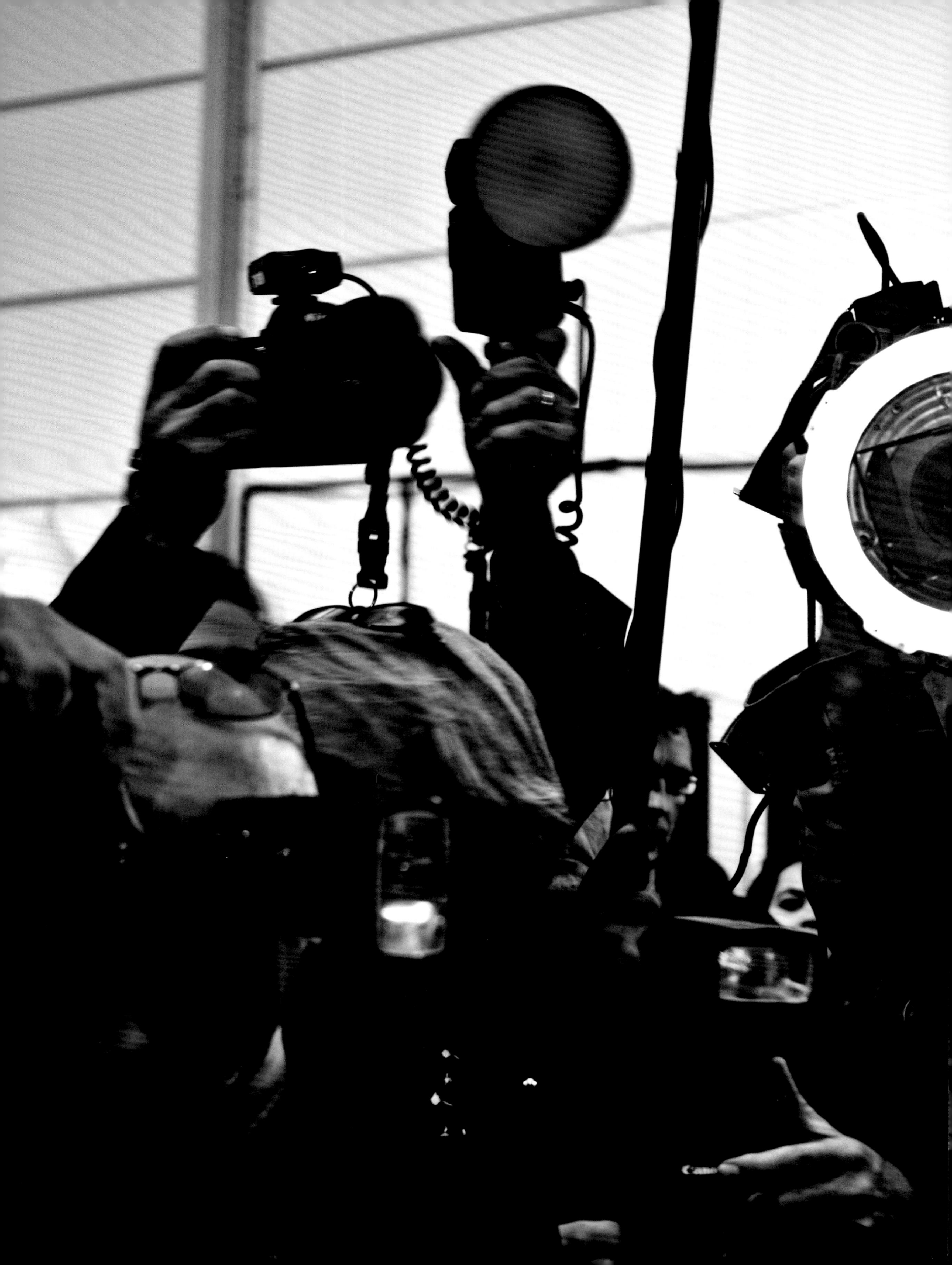

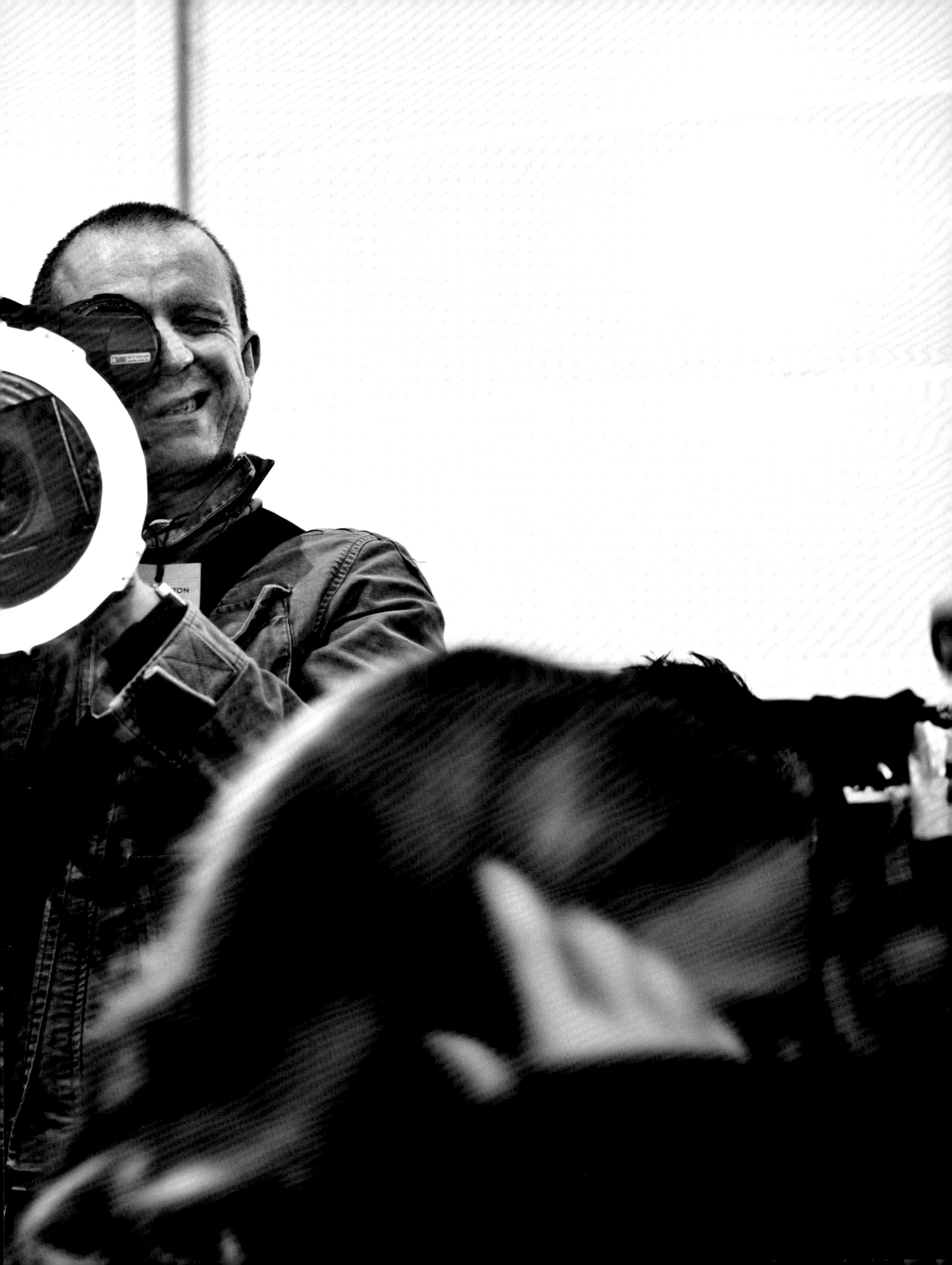

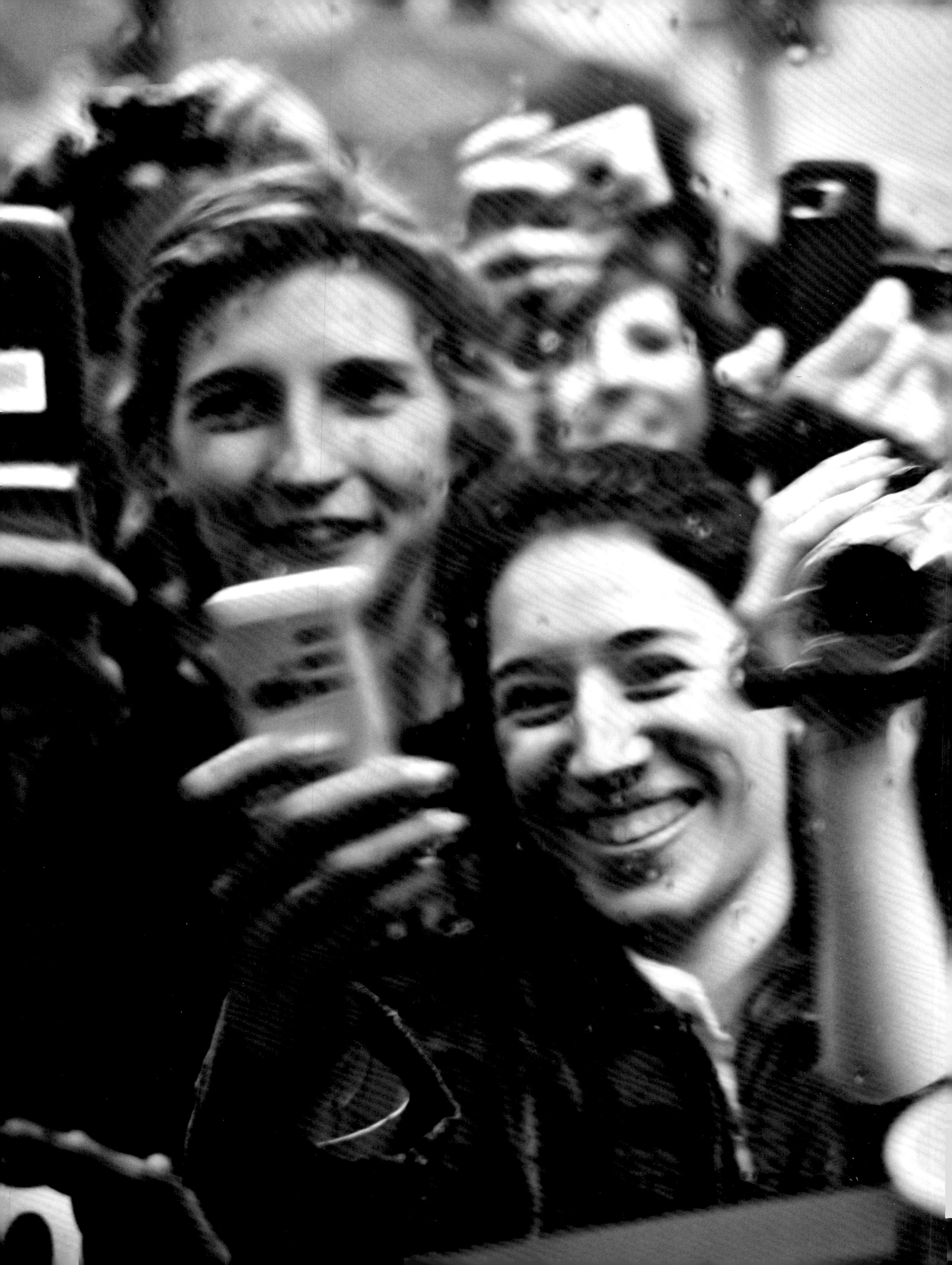

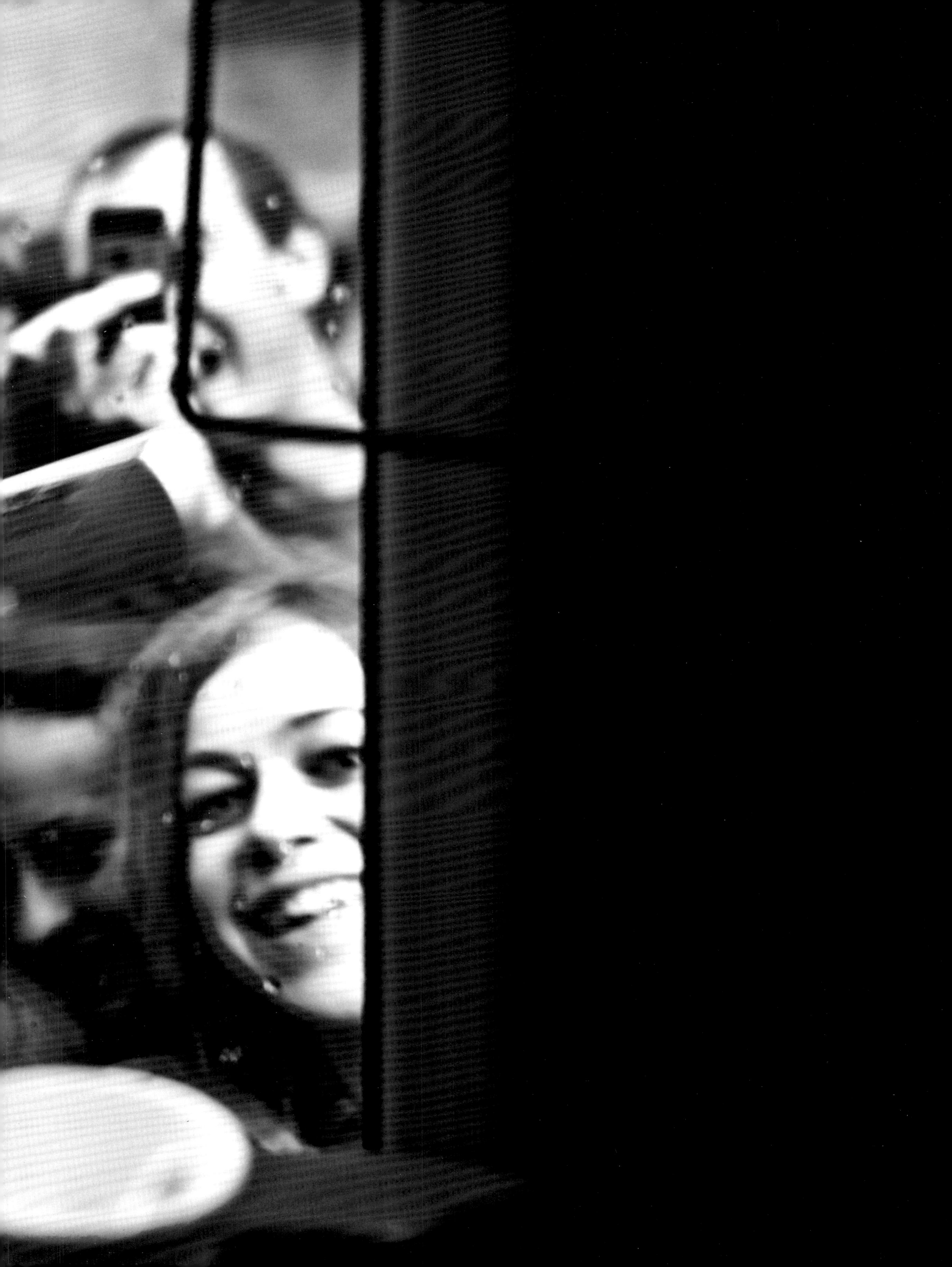

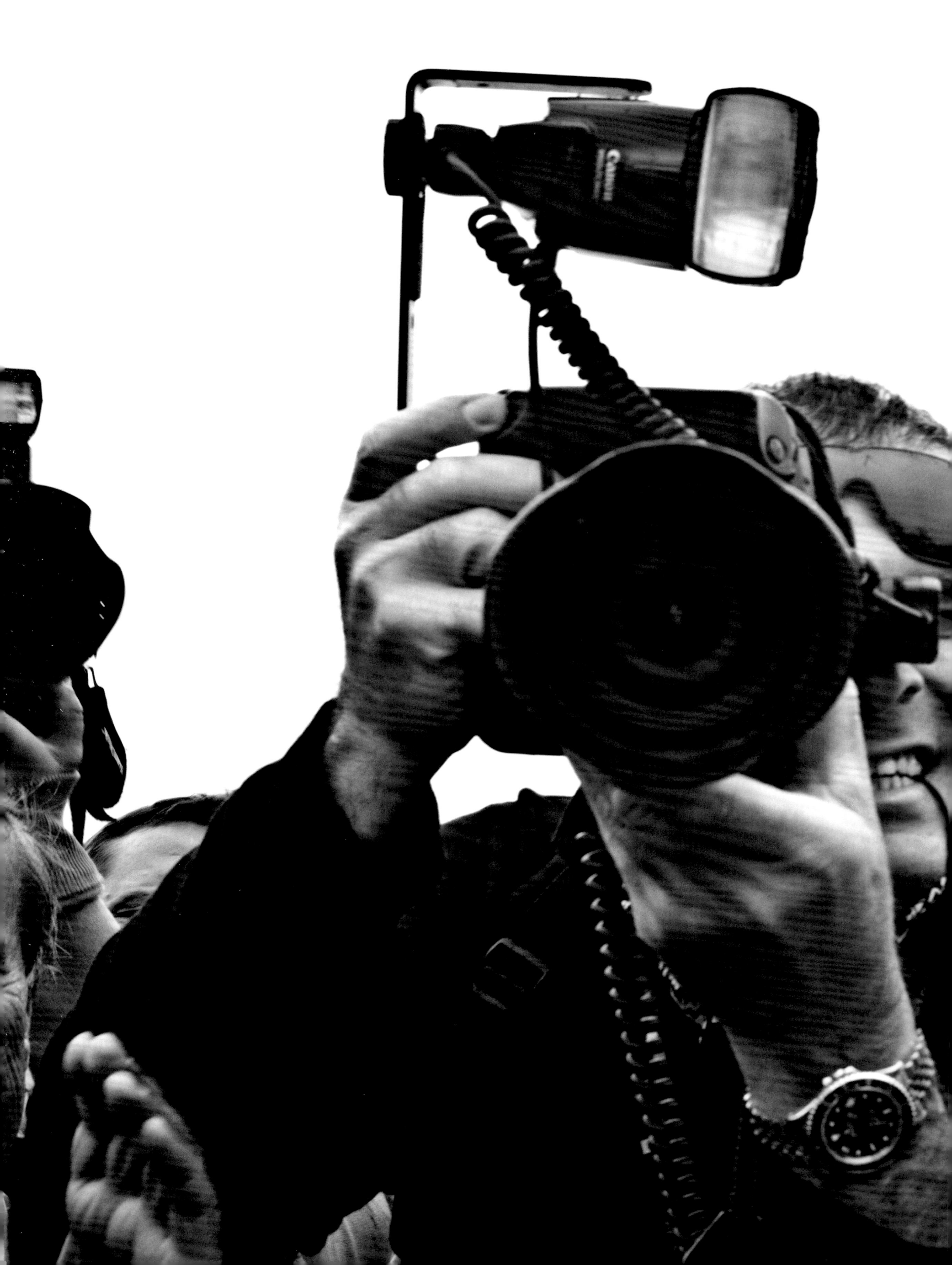

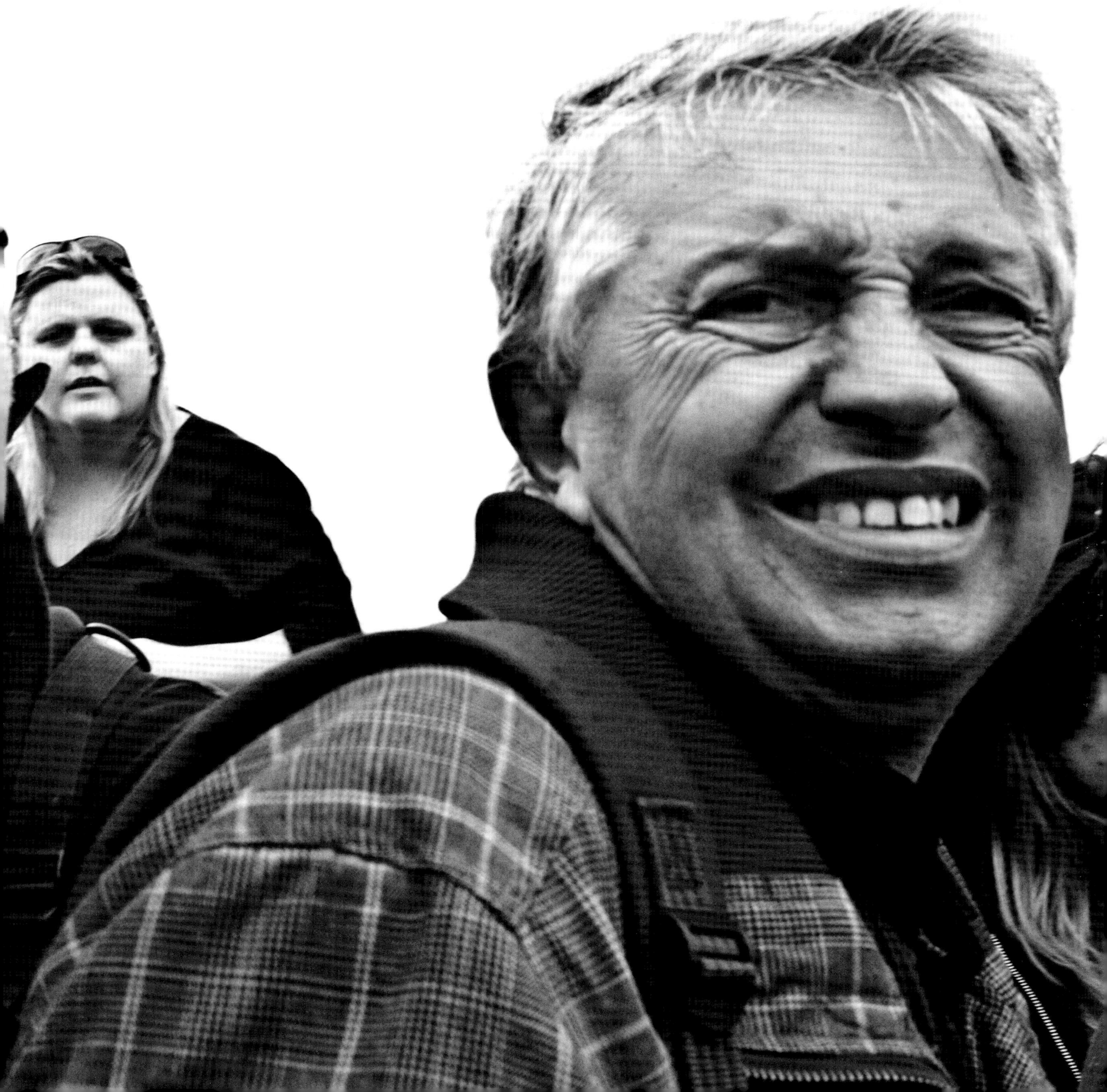

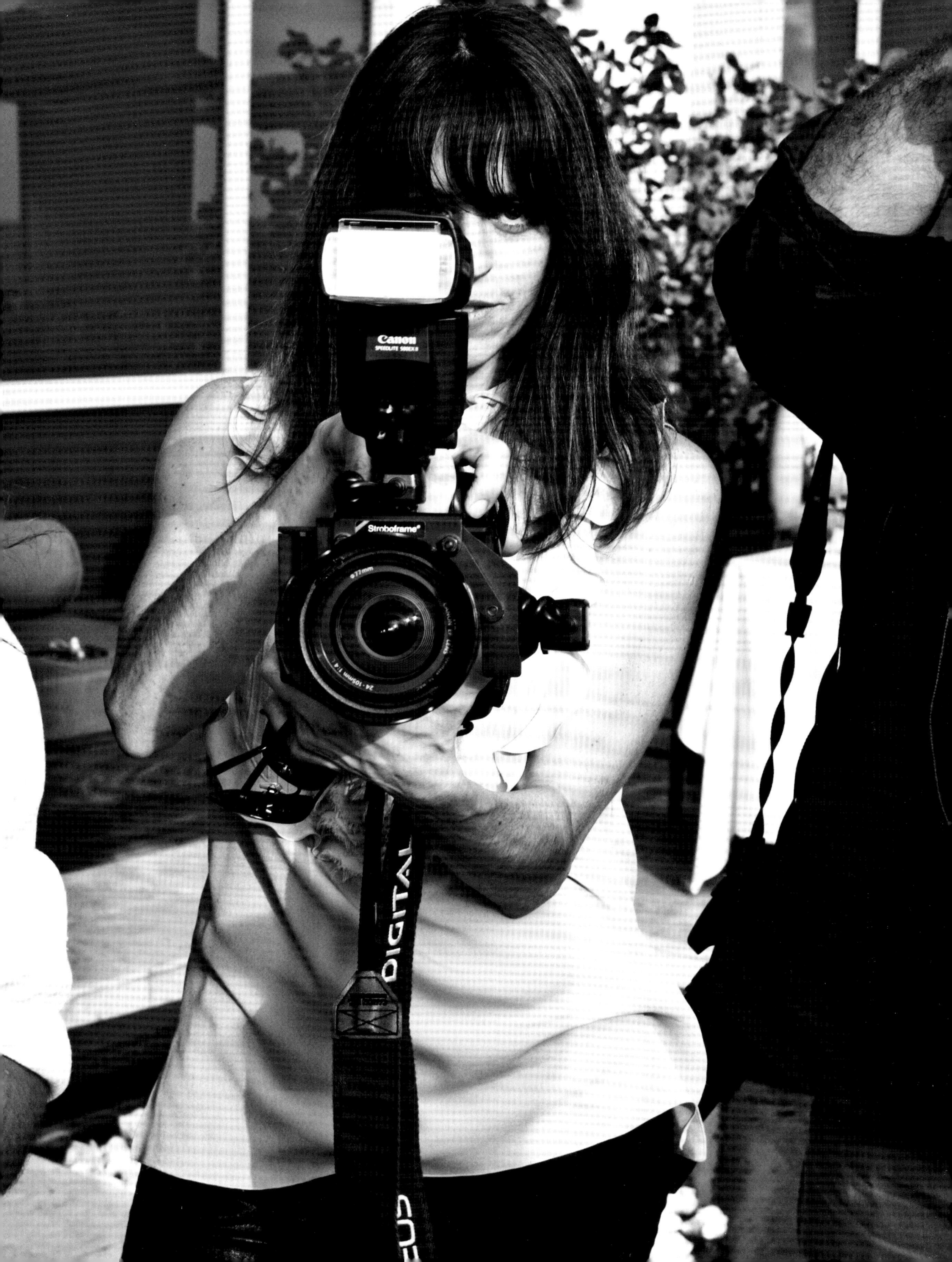
Canon
Stroboframe
DIGITAL

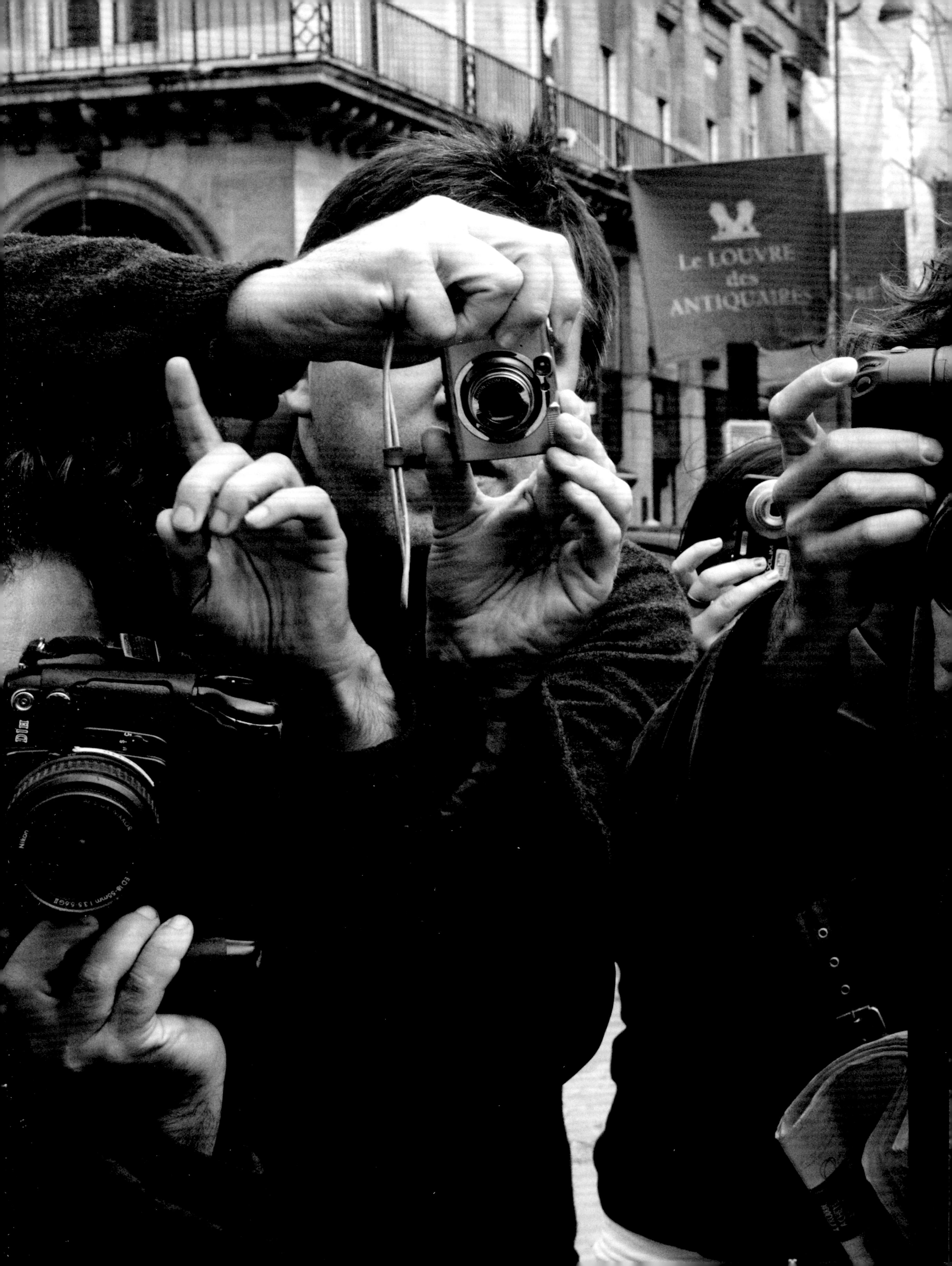
Le LOUVRE
des
ANTIQUAIRES

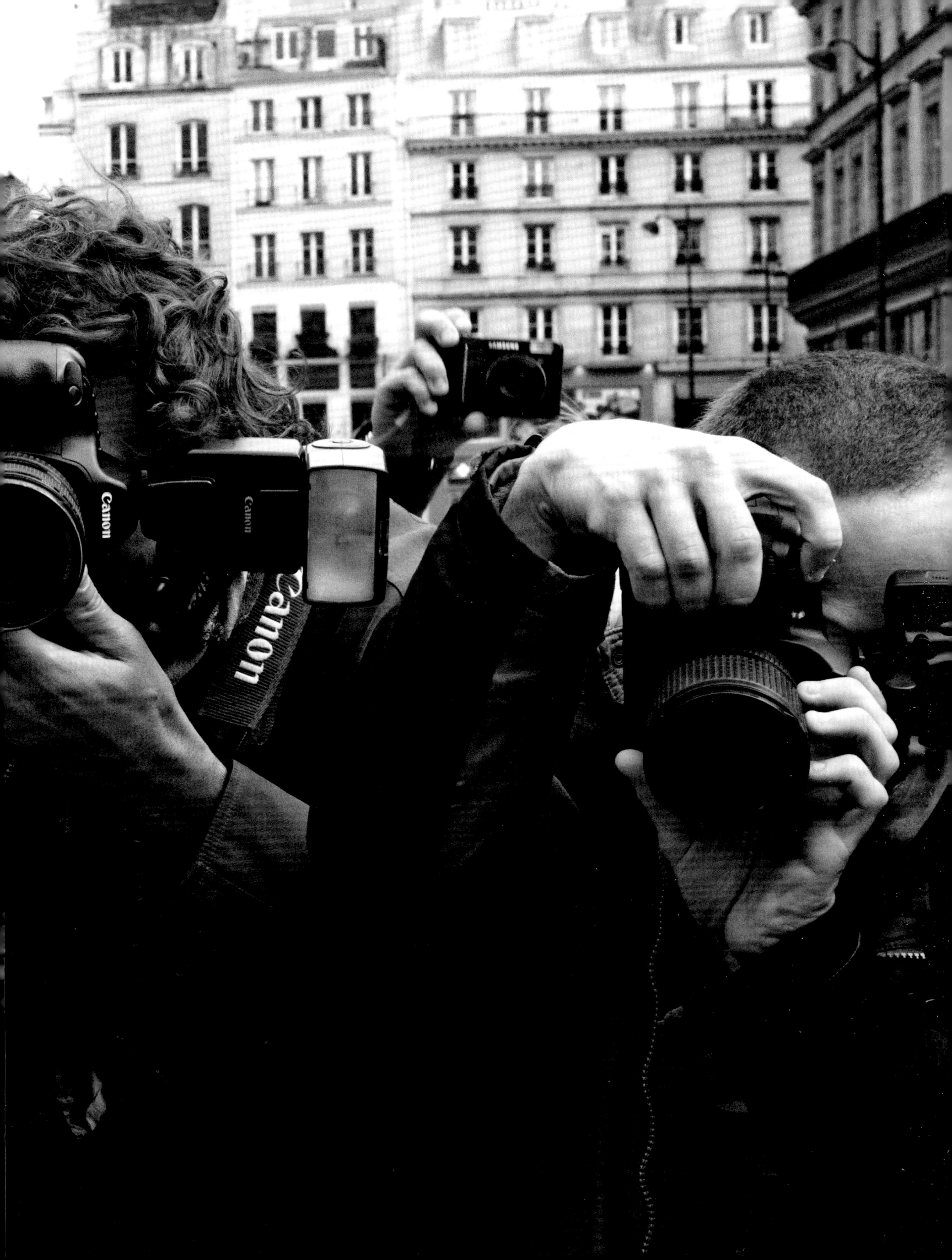
Canon
Canon
Canon
Canon

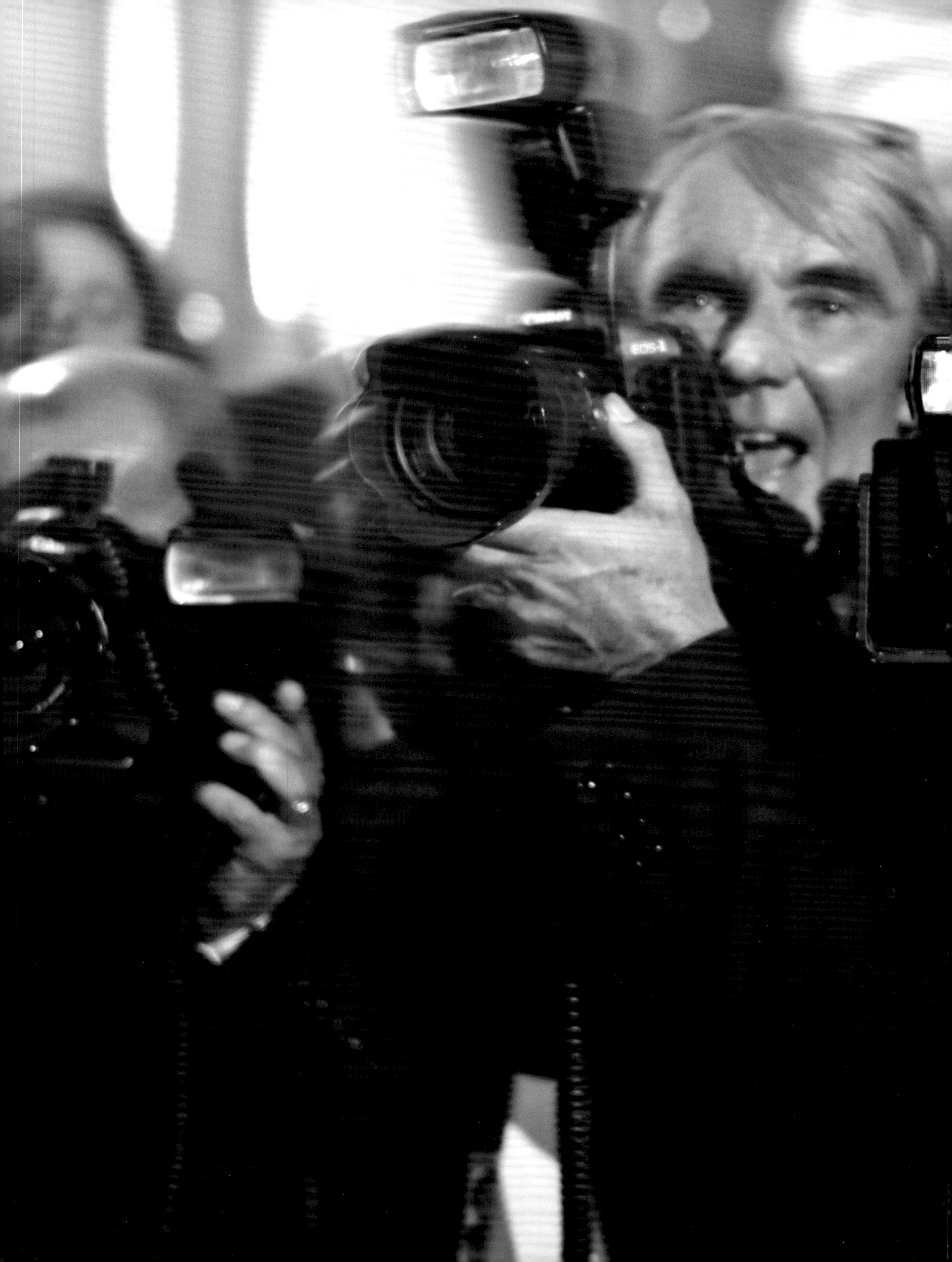

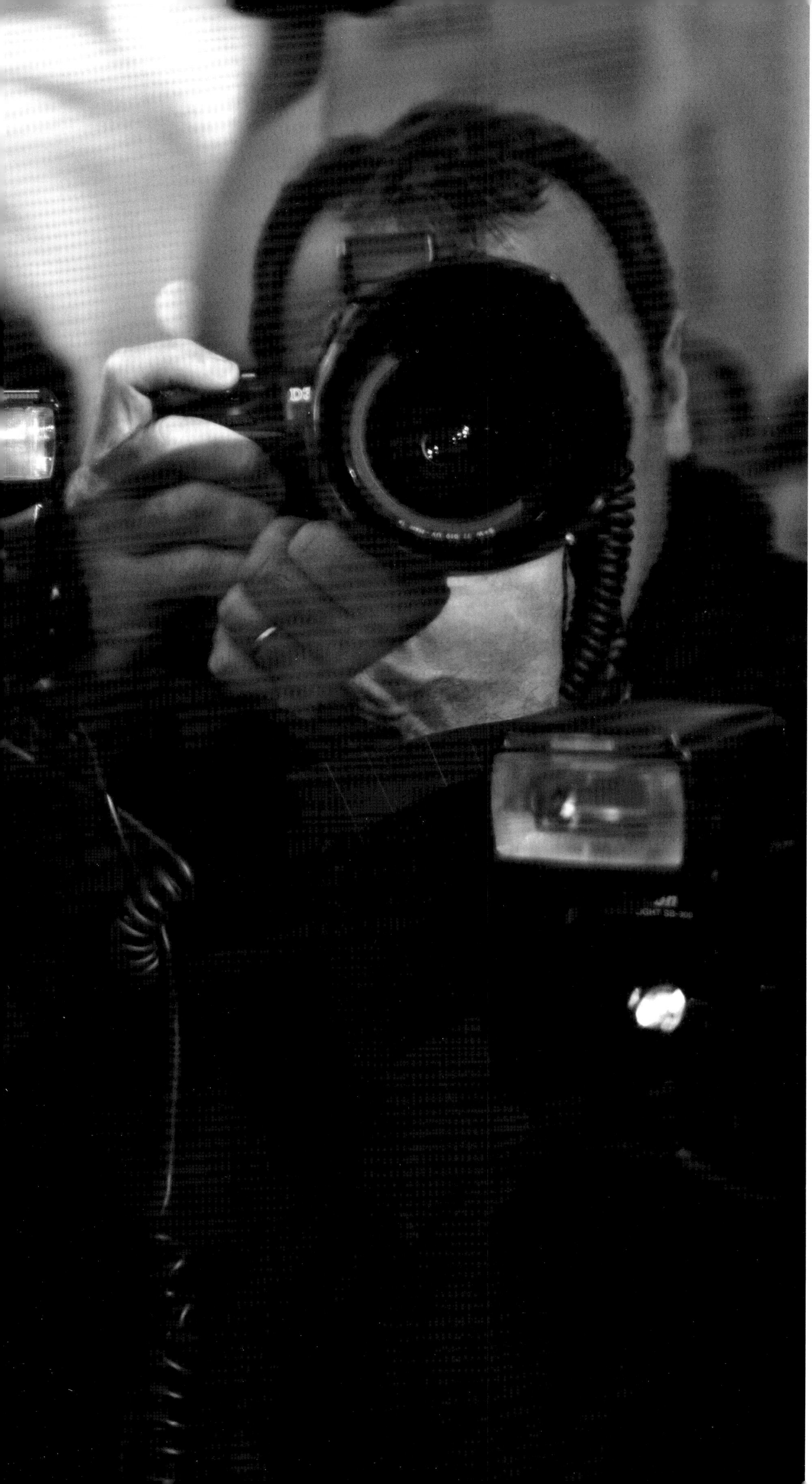

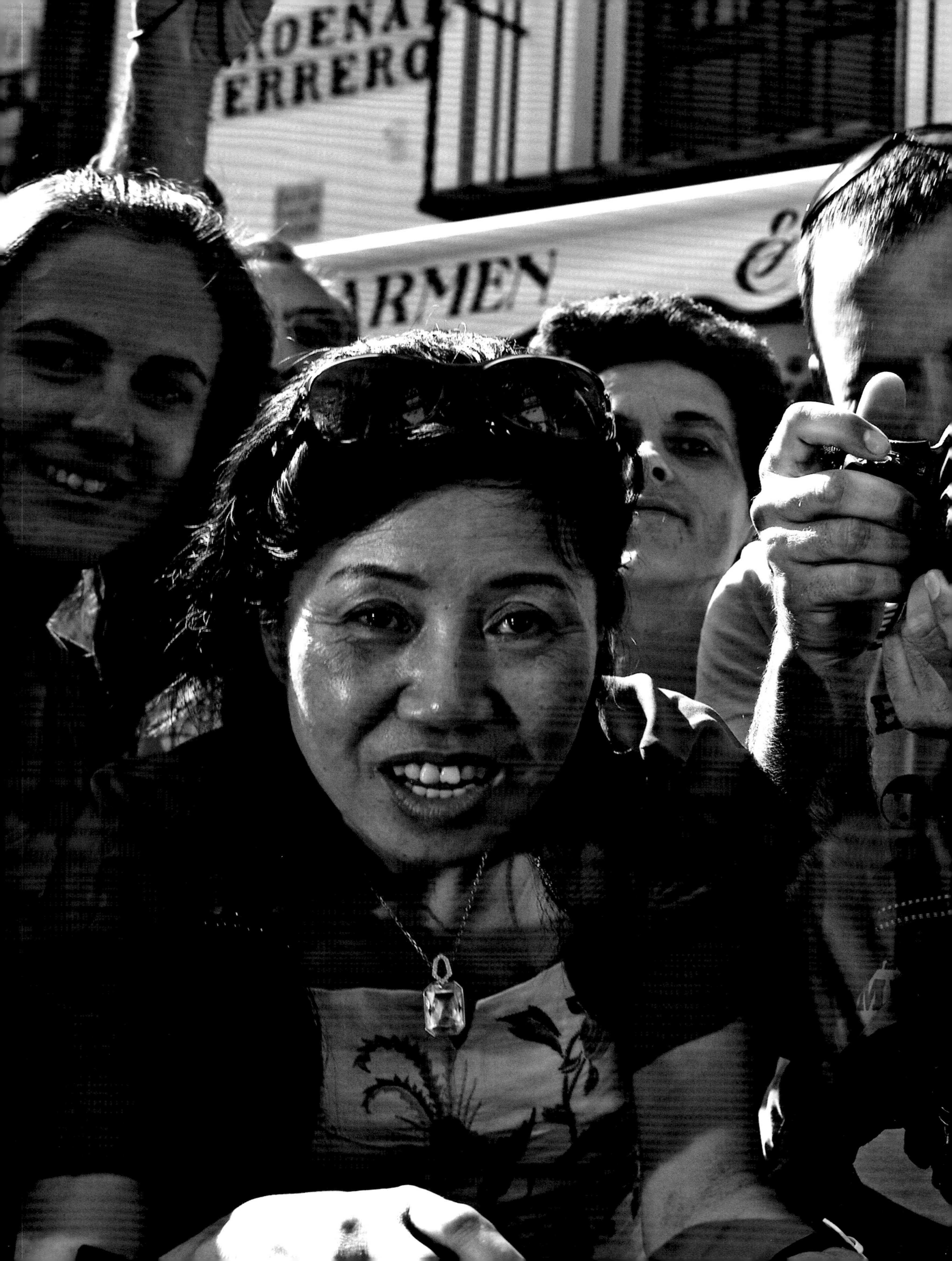
ERRERO
ARMEN

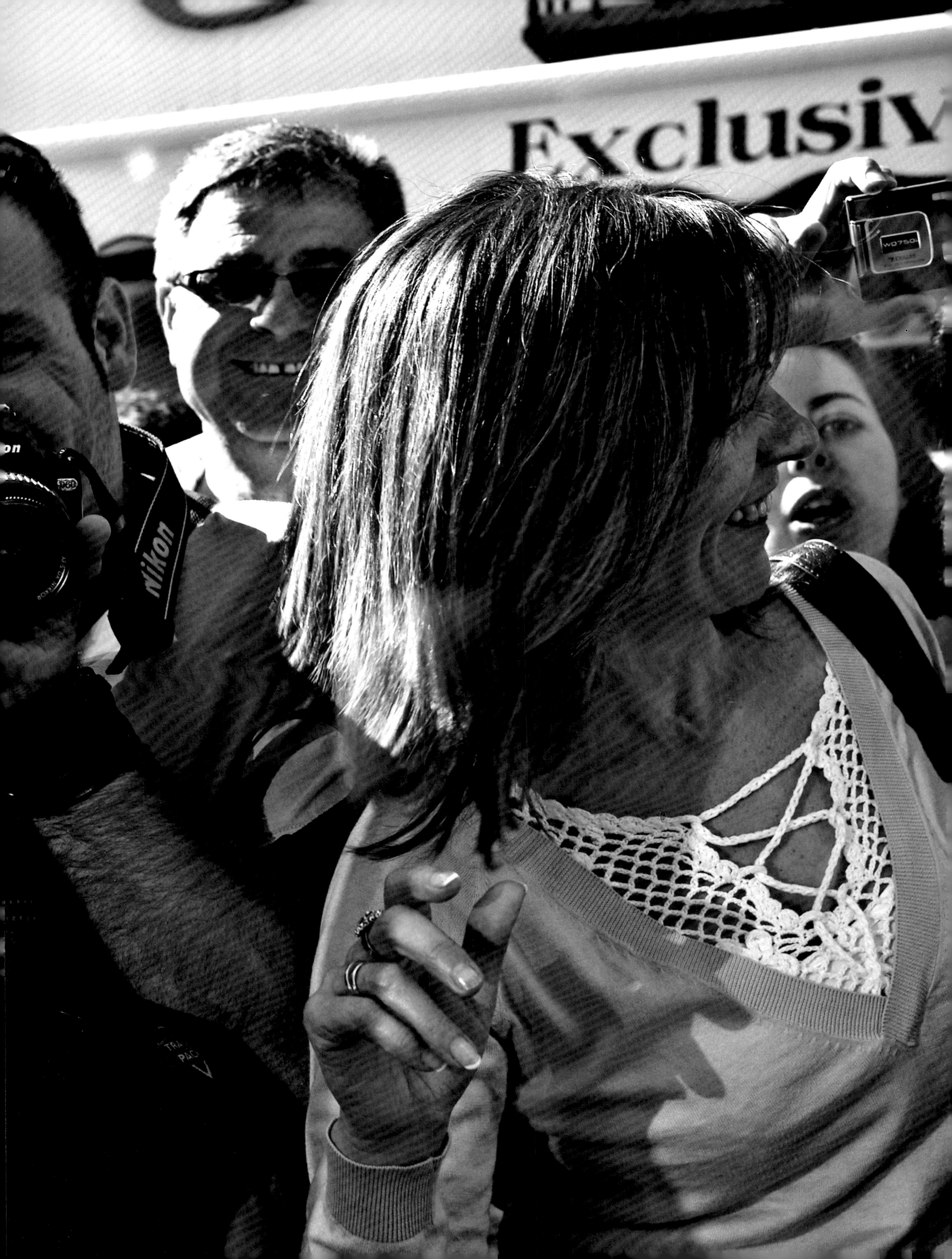
Exclusiv
Nikon

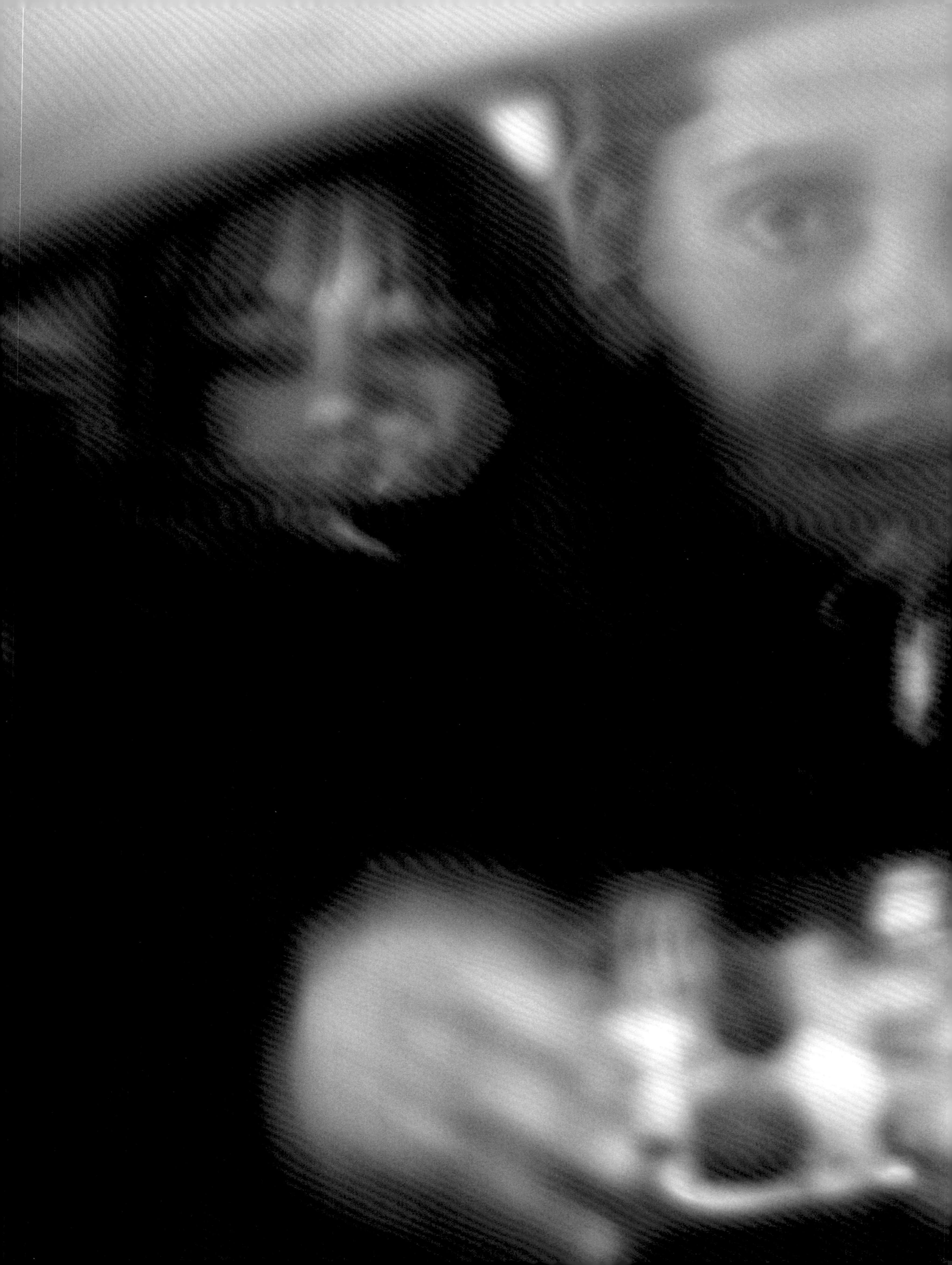

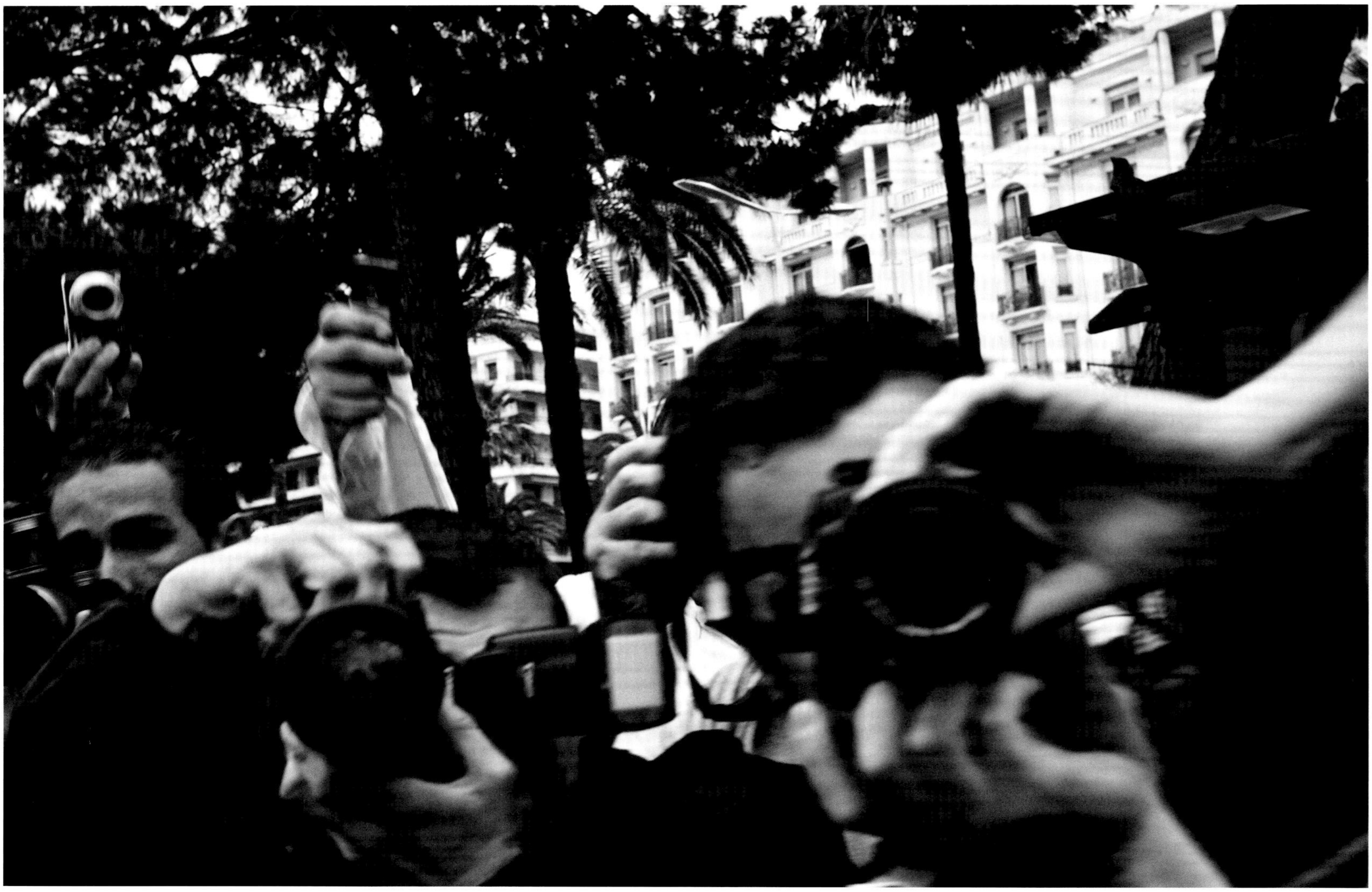

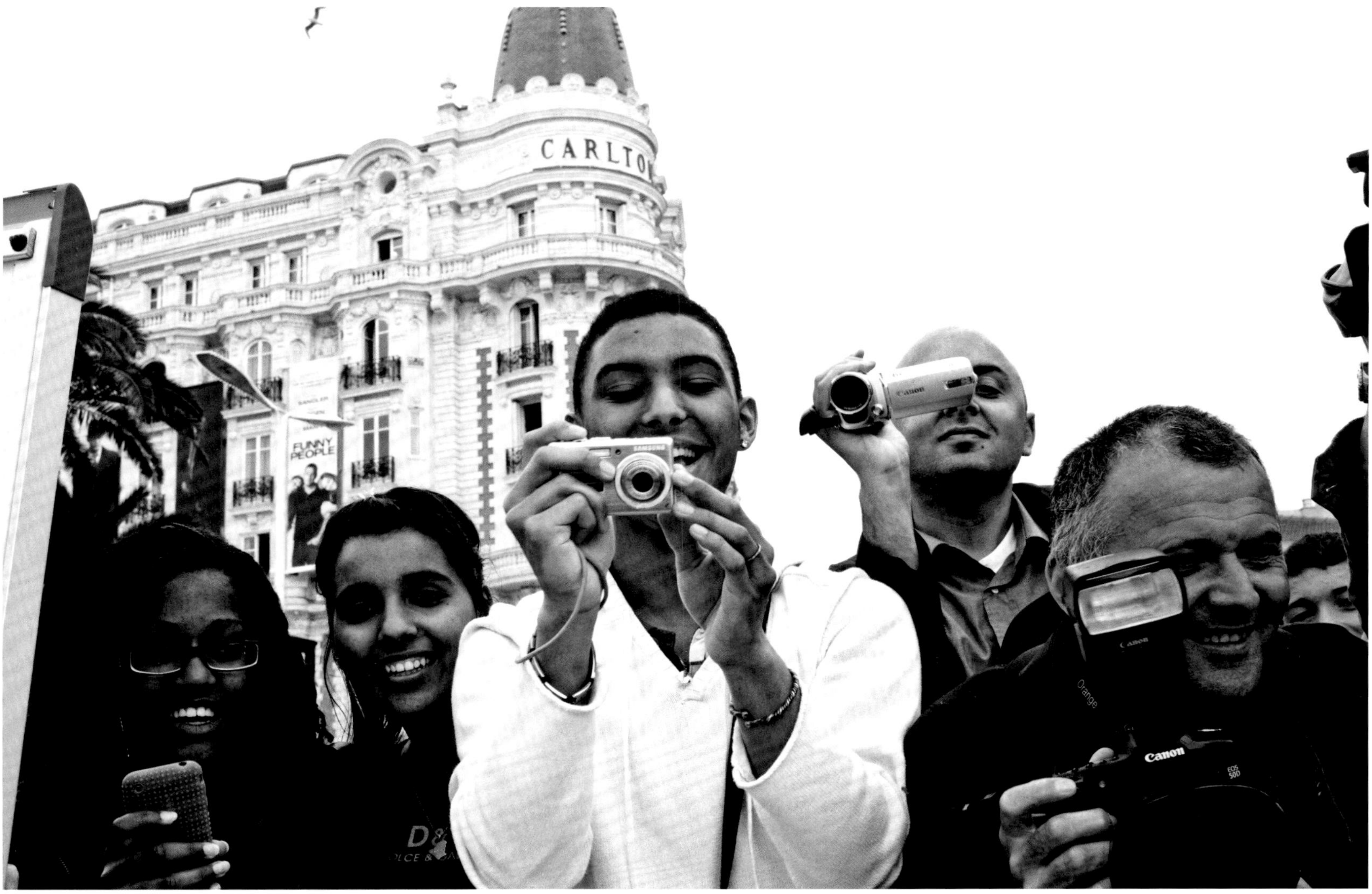
CARLTO
FUNNY PEOPLE
Canon

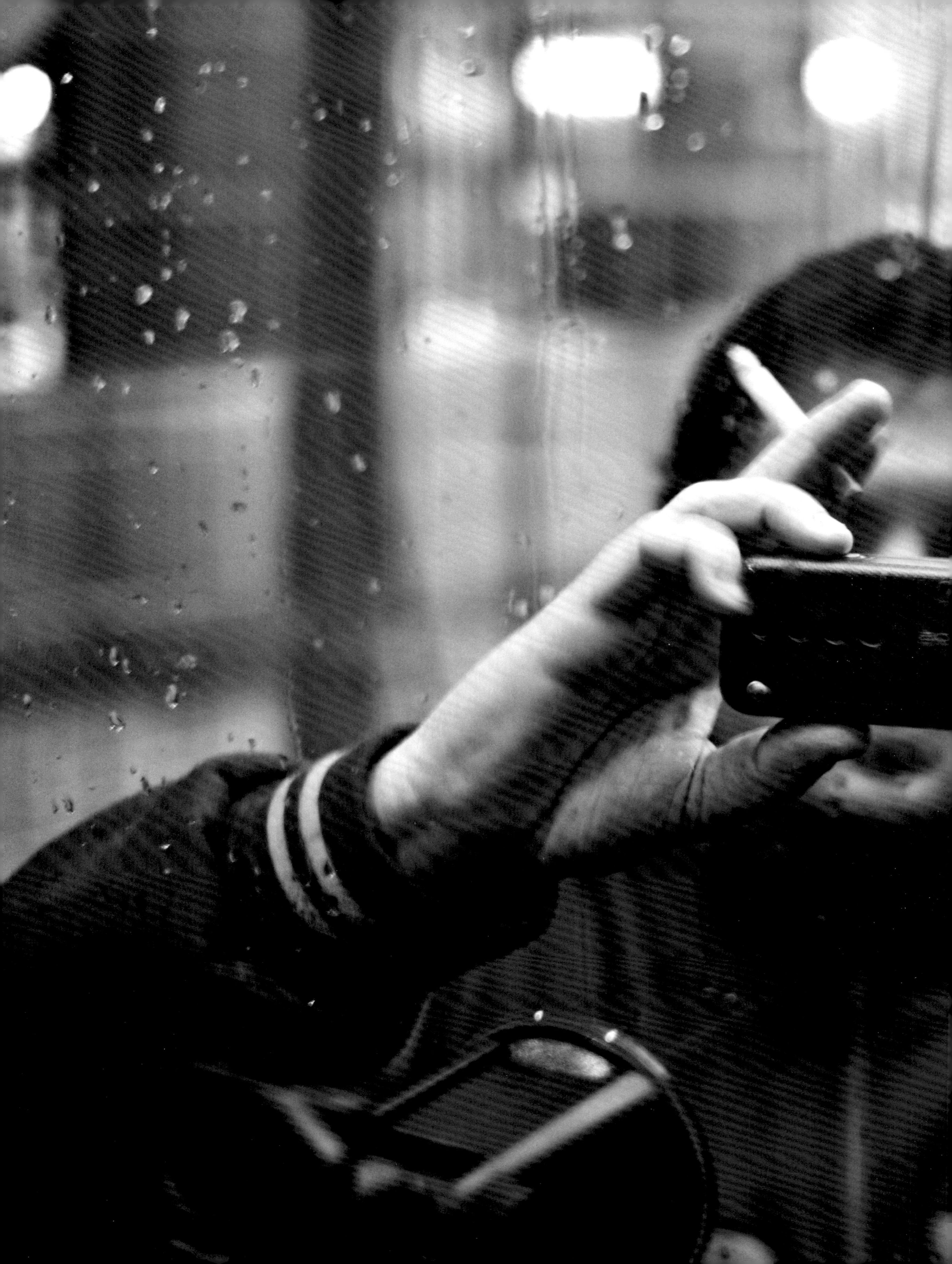

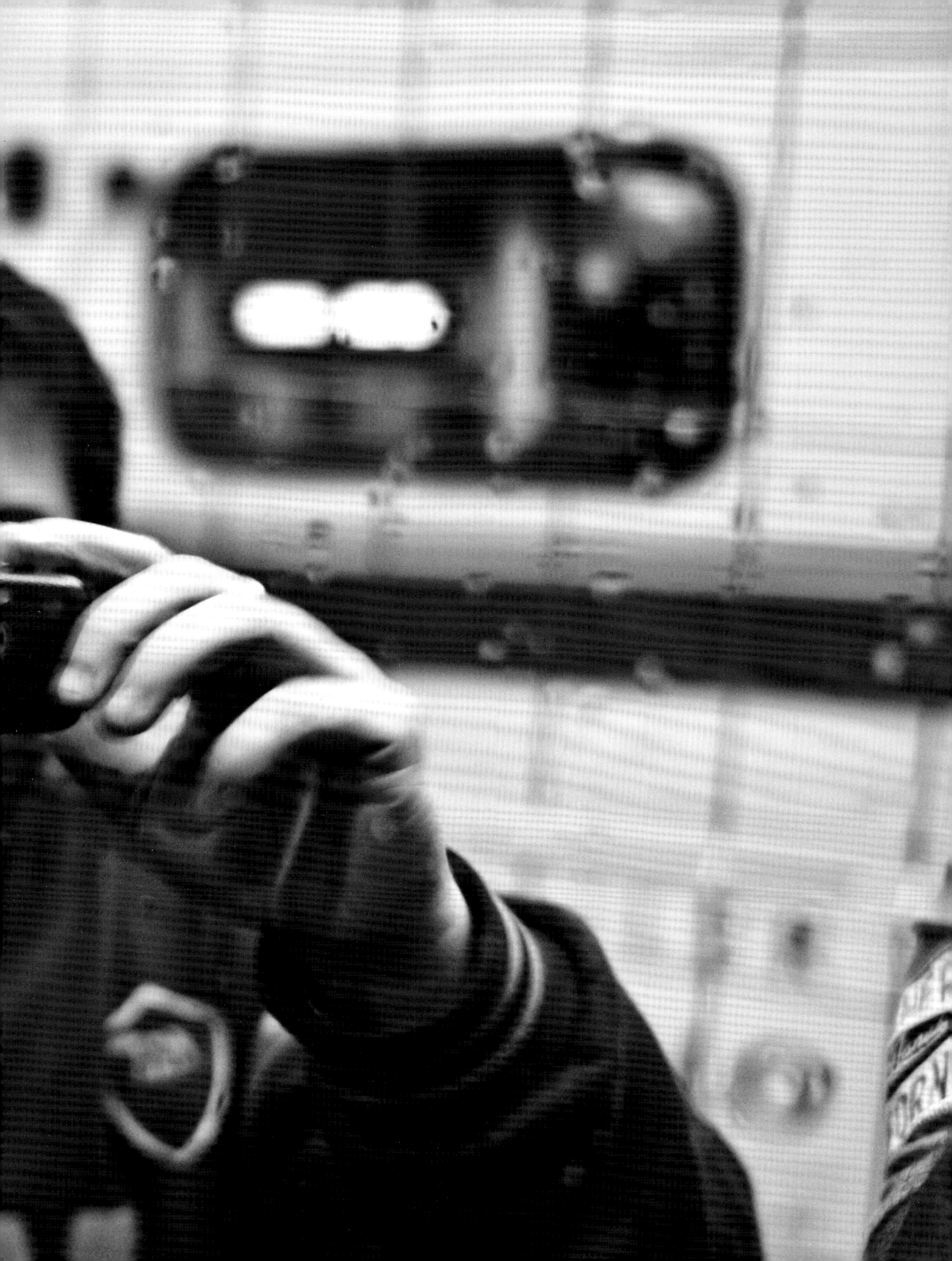

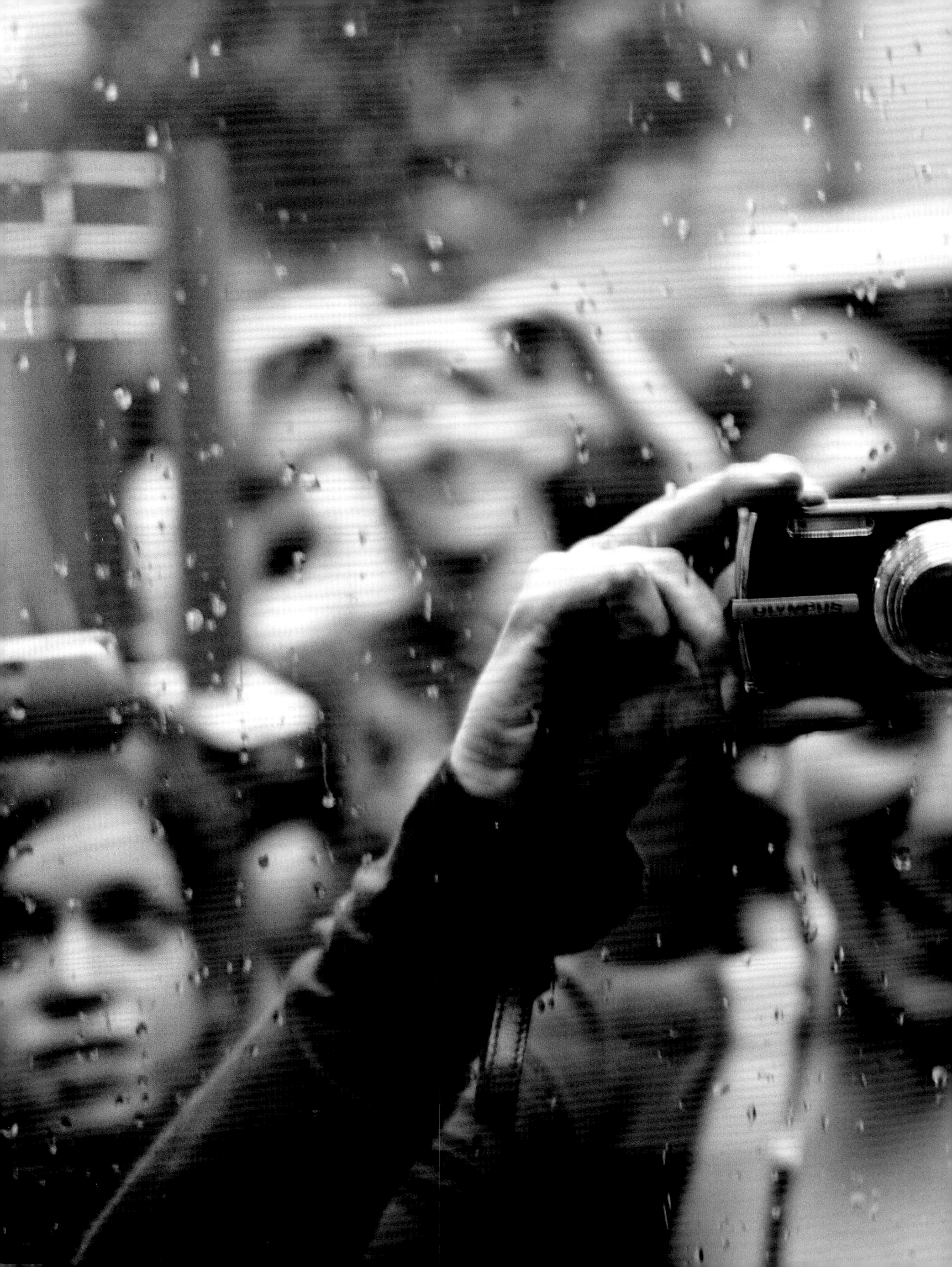

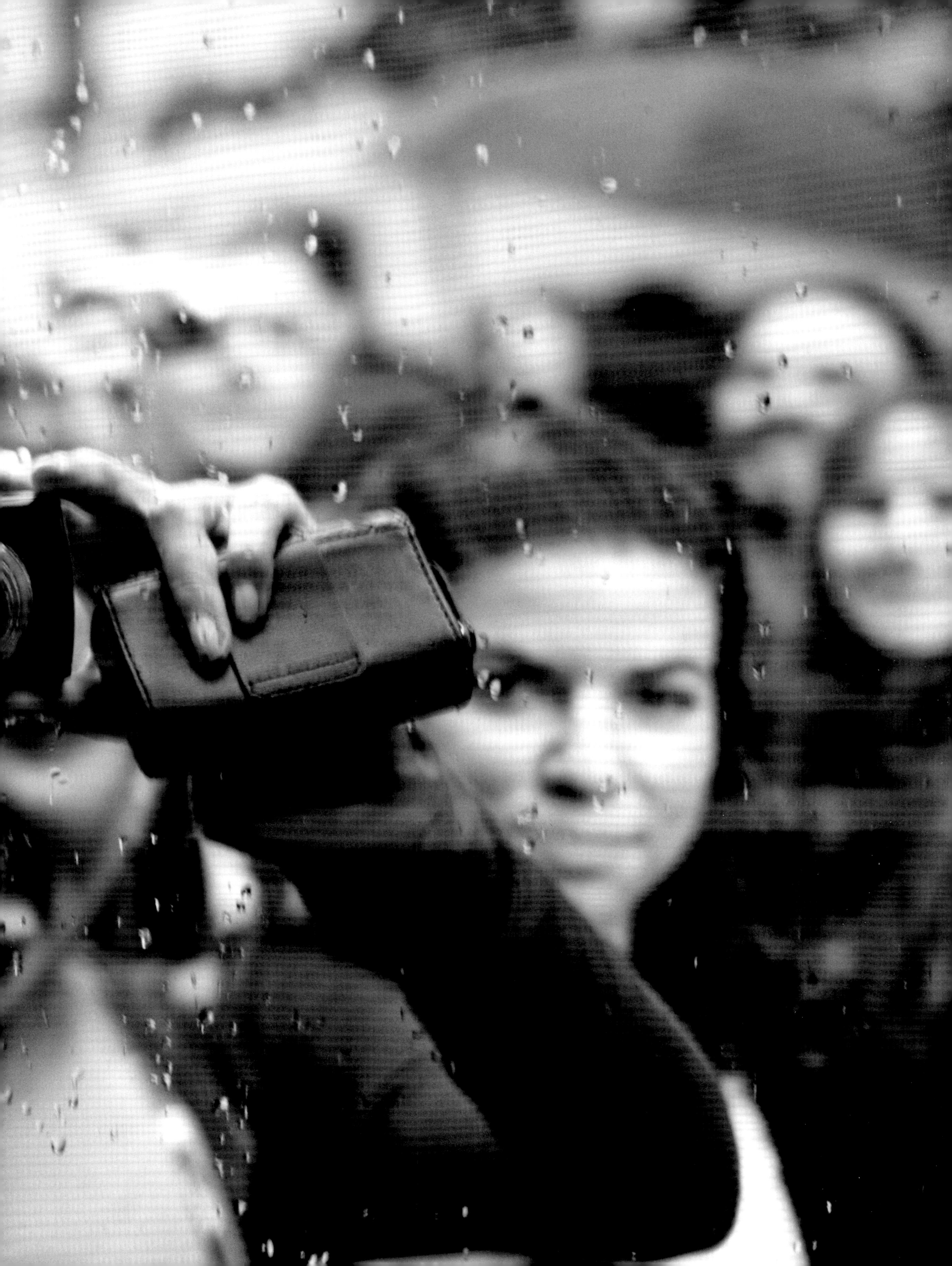

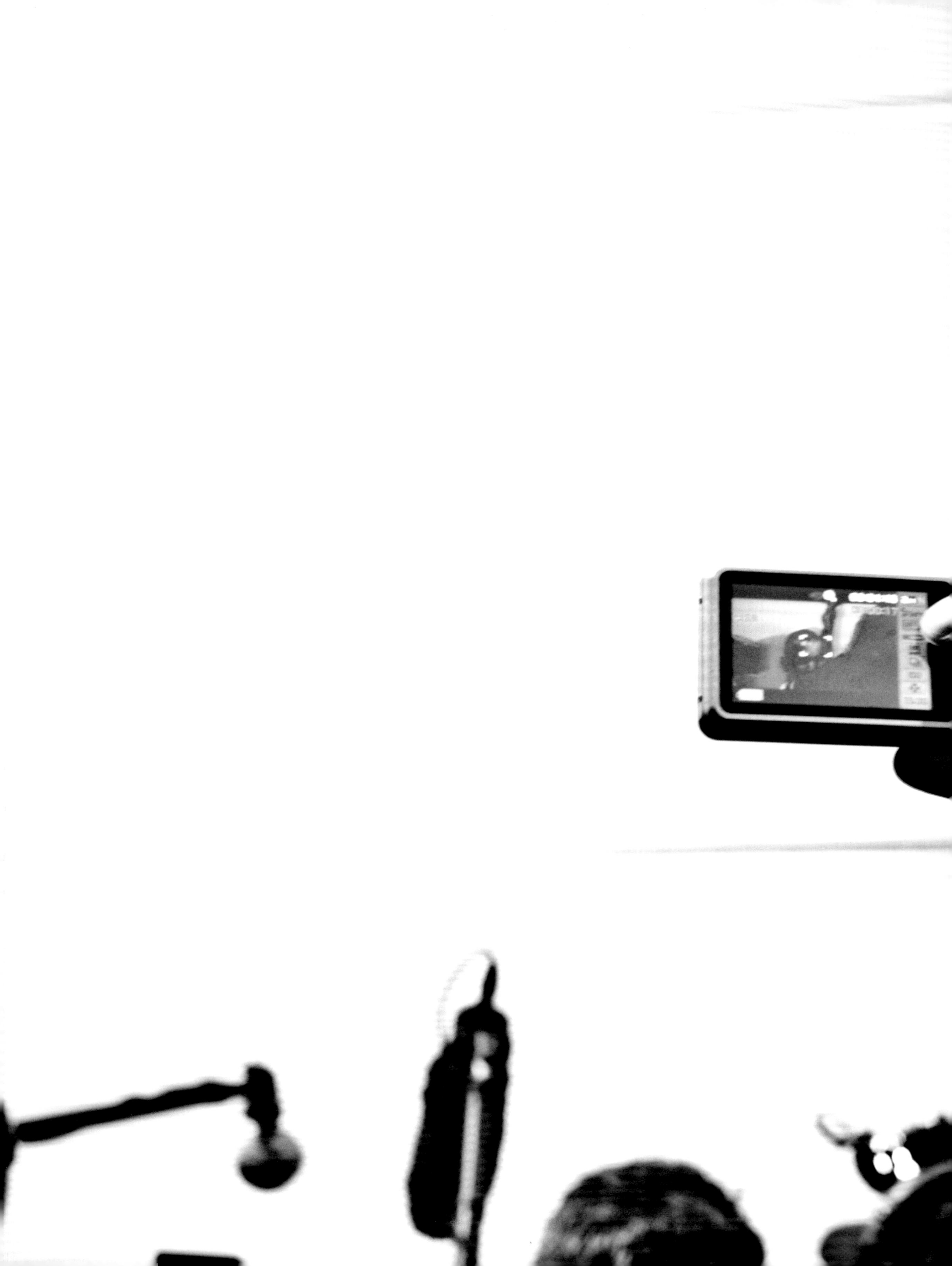

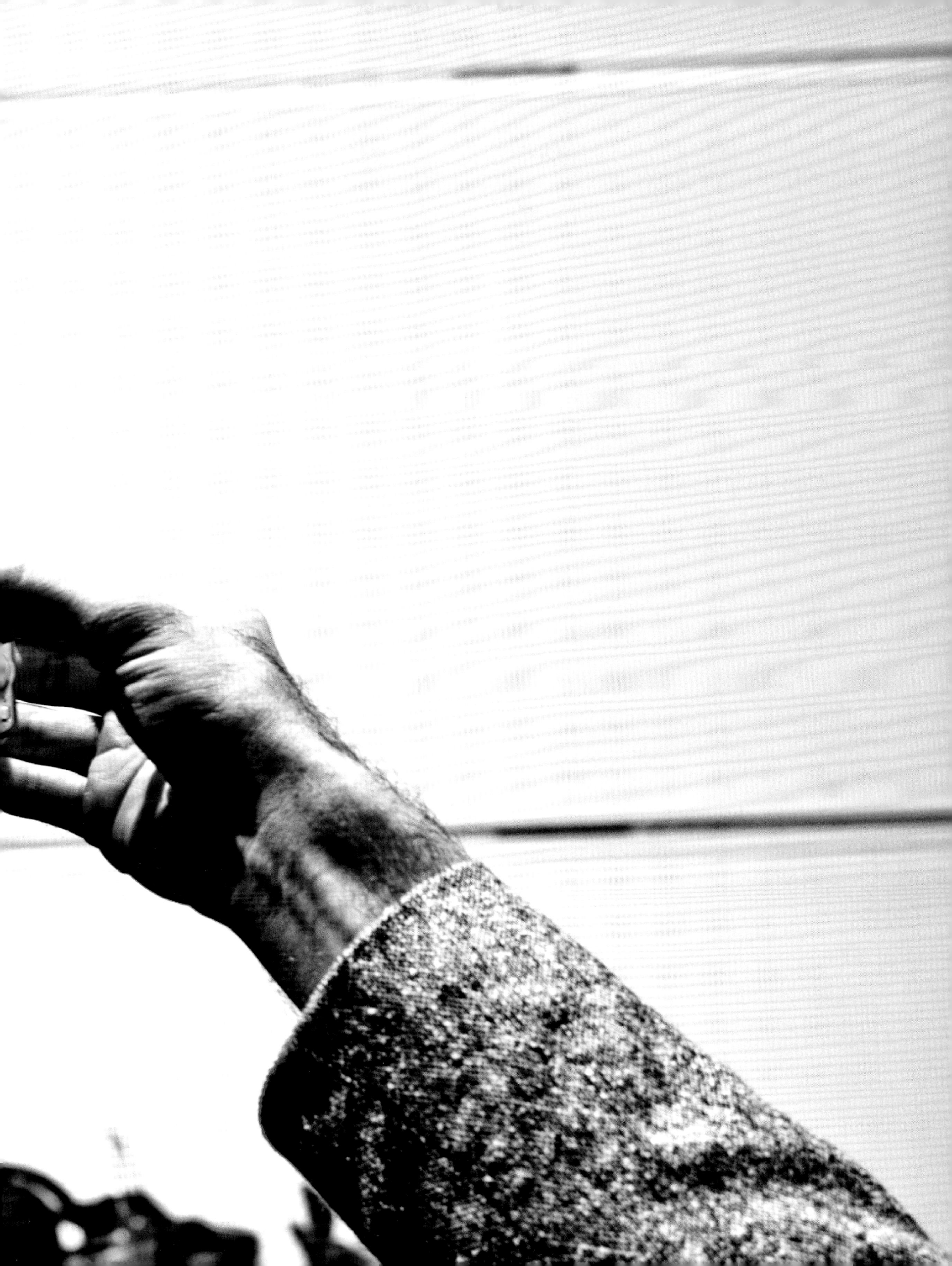

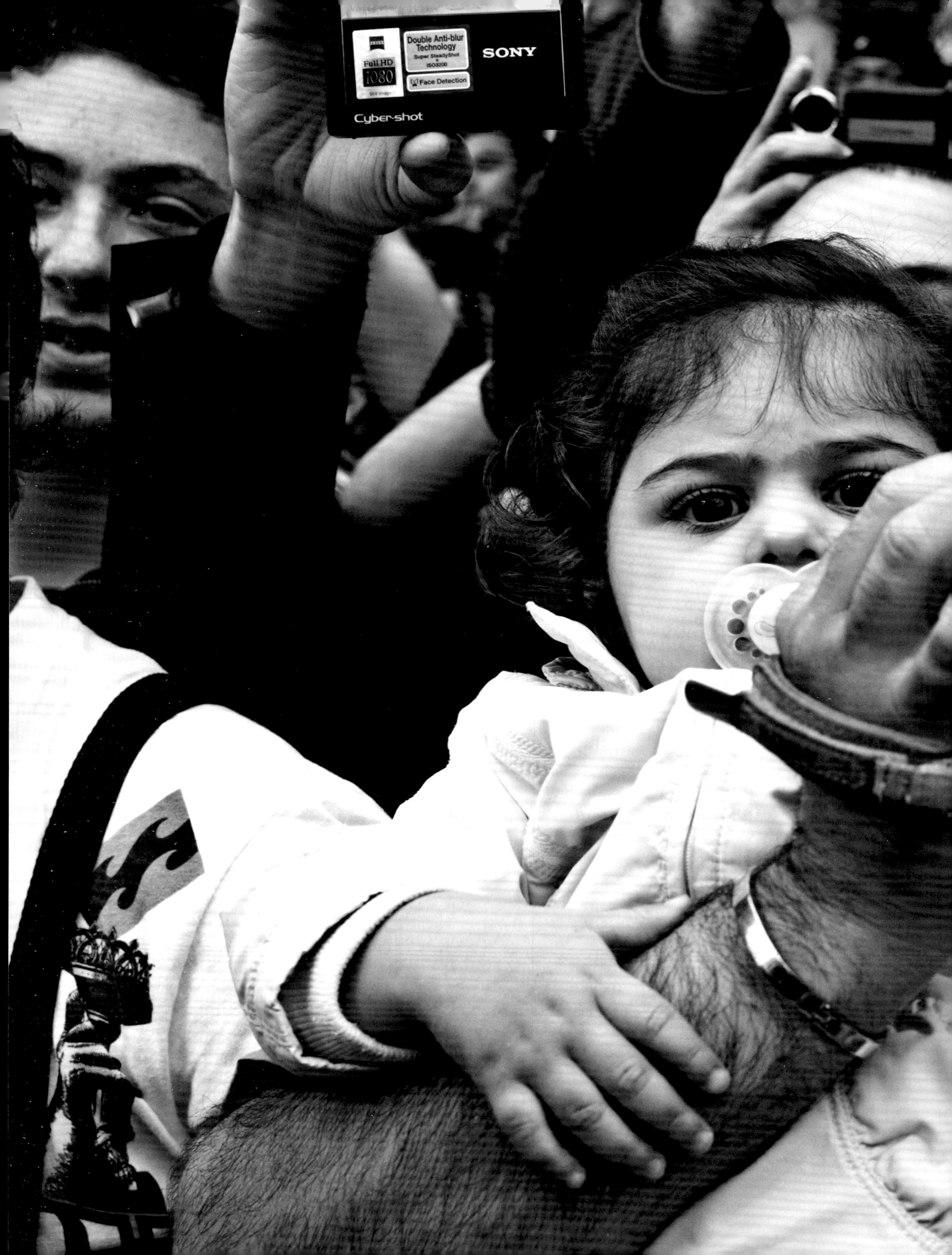
ZEISS
Full HD
1080
Double Anti-blur
Technology
Super SteadyShot
ISO3200
Face Detection
SONY
Cyber-shot

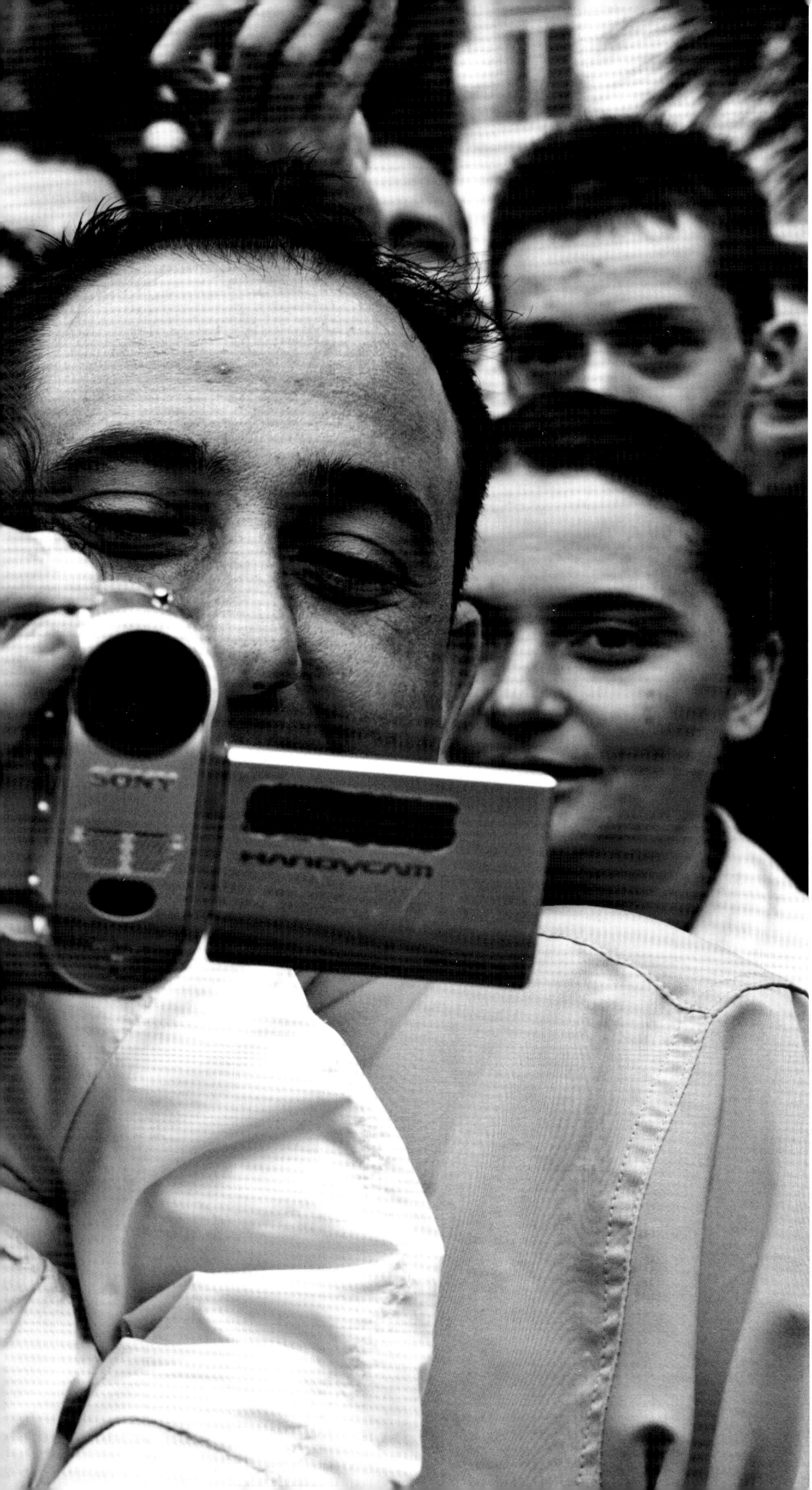
SONY
HANDYCAM

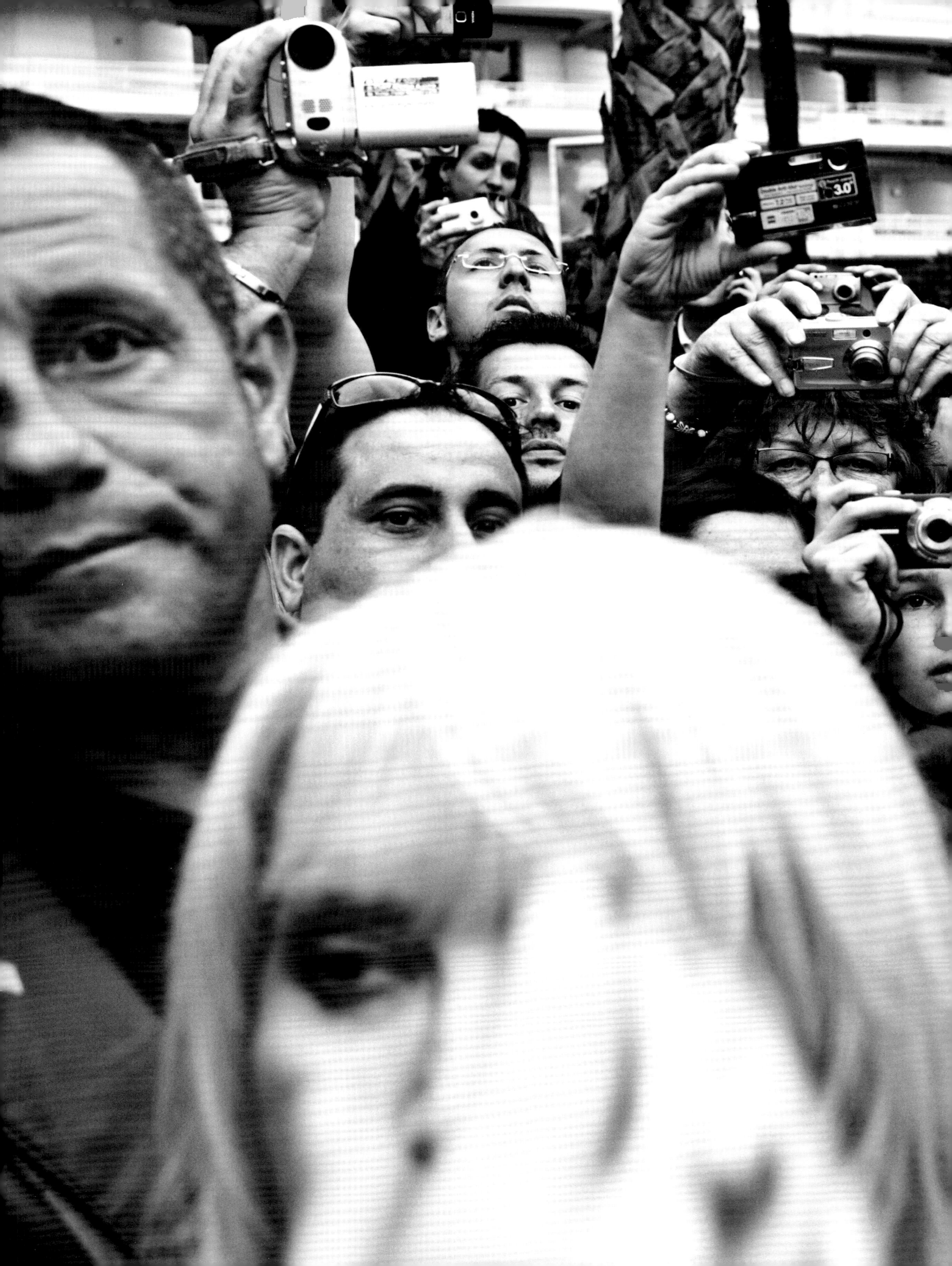
3.0

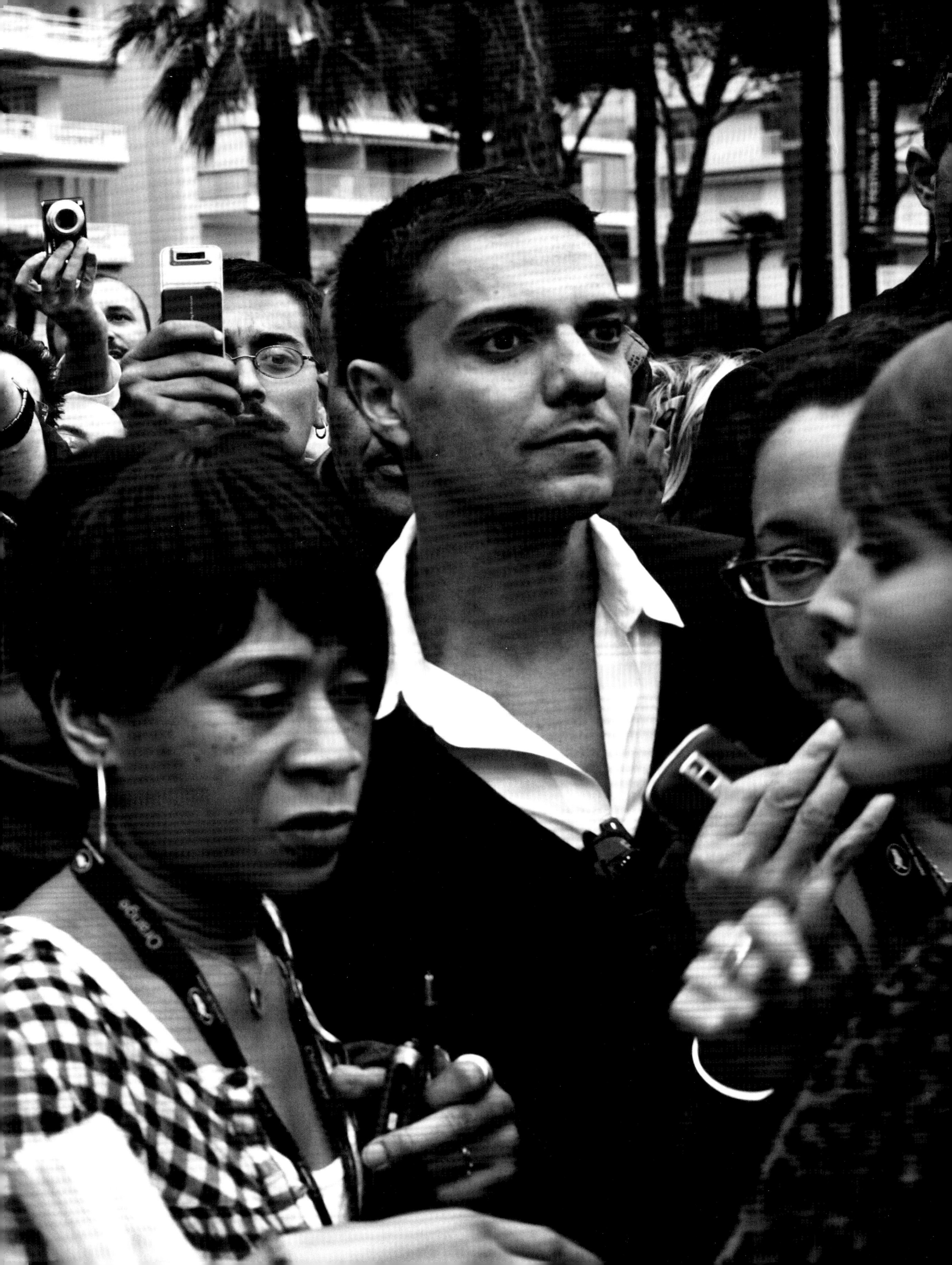

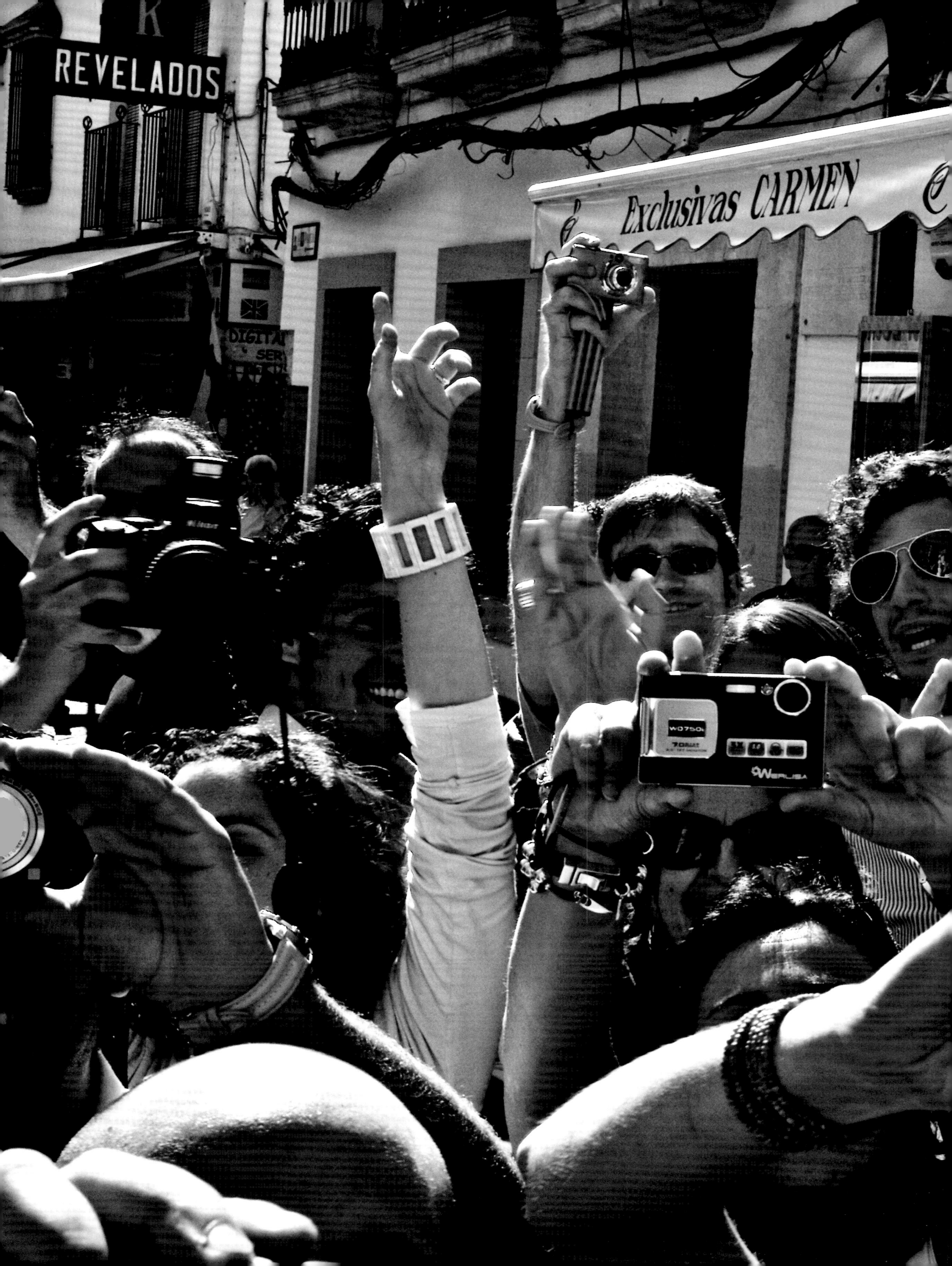
REVELADOS
Exclusivas CARMEN

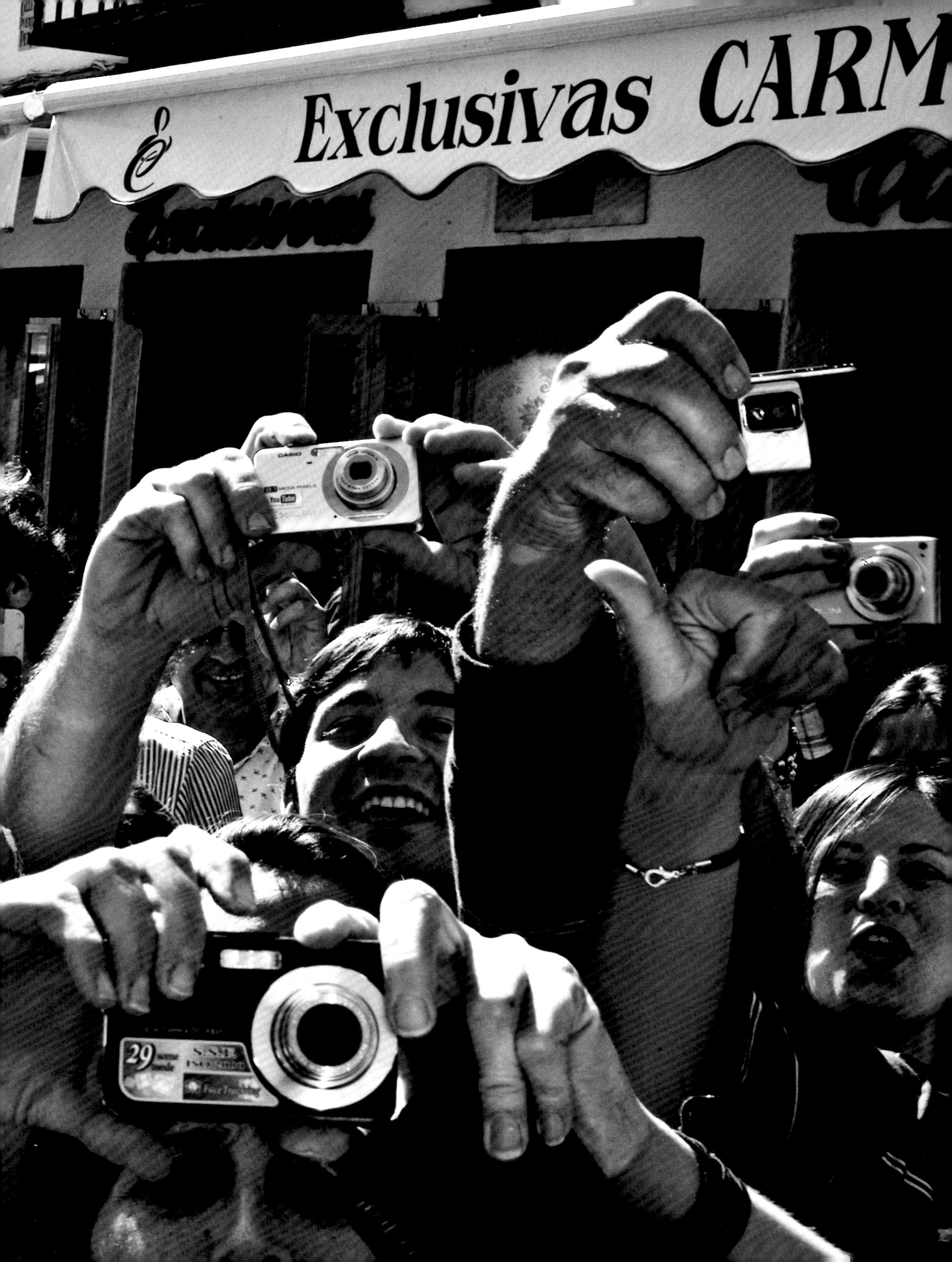
Exclusivas CARM

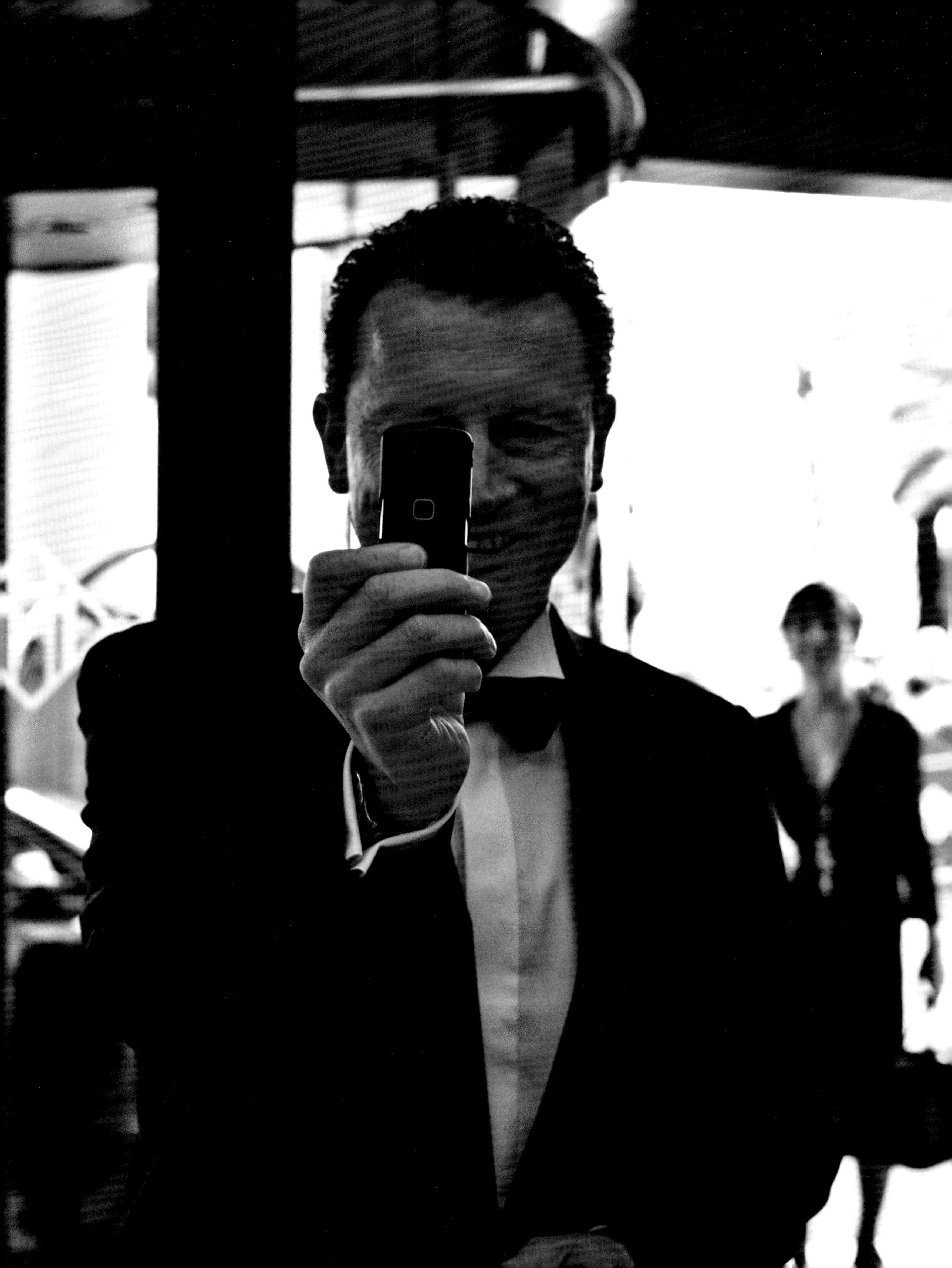

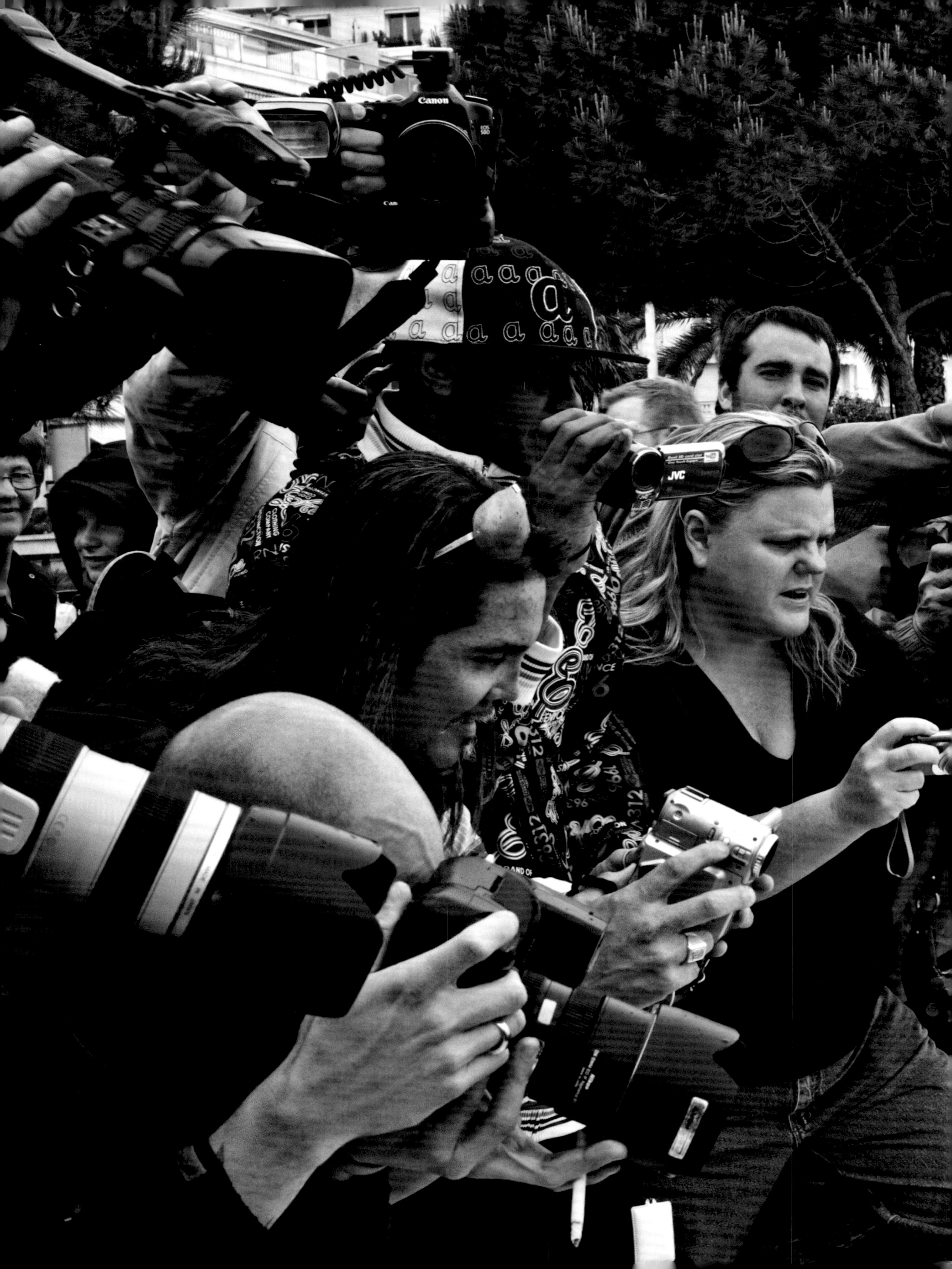
Canon
JVC

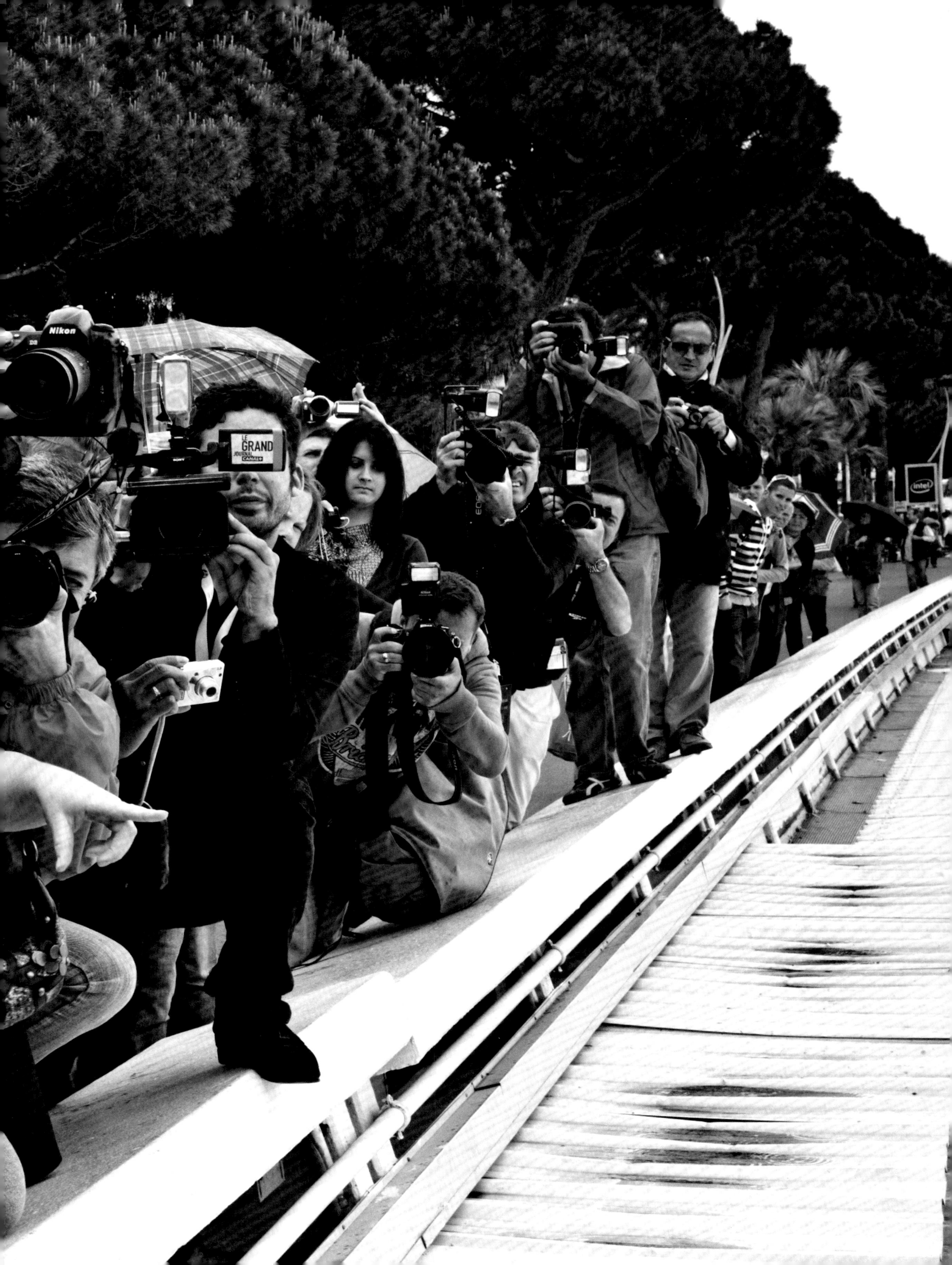
Nikon
LE GRAND
JOURNAL
CANAL+
intel

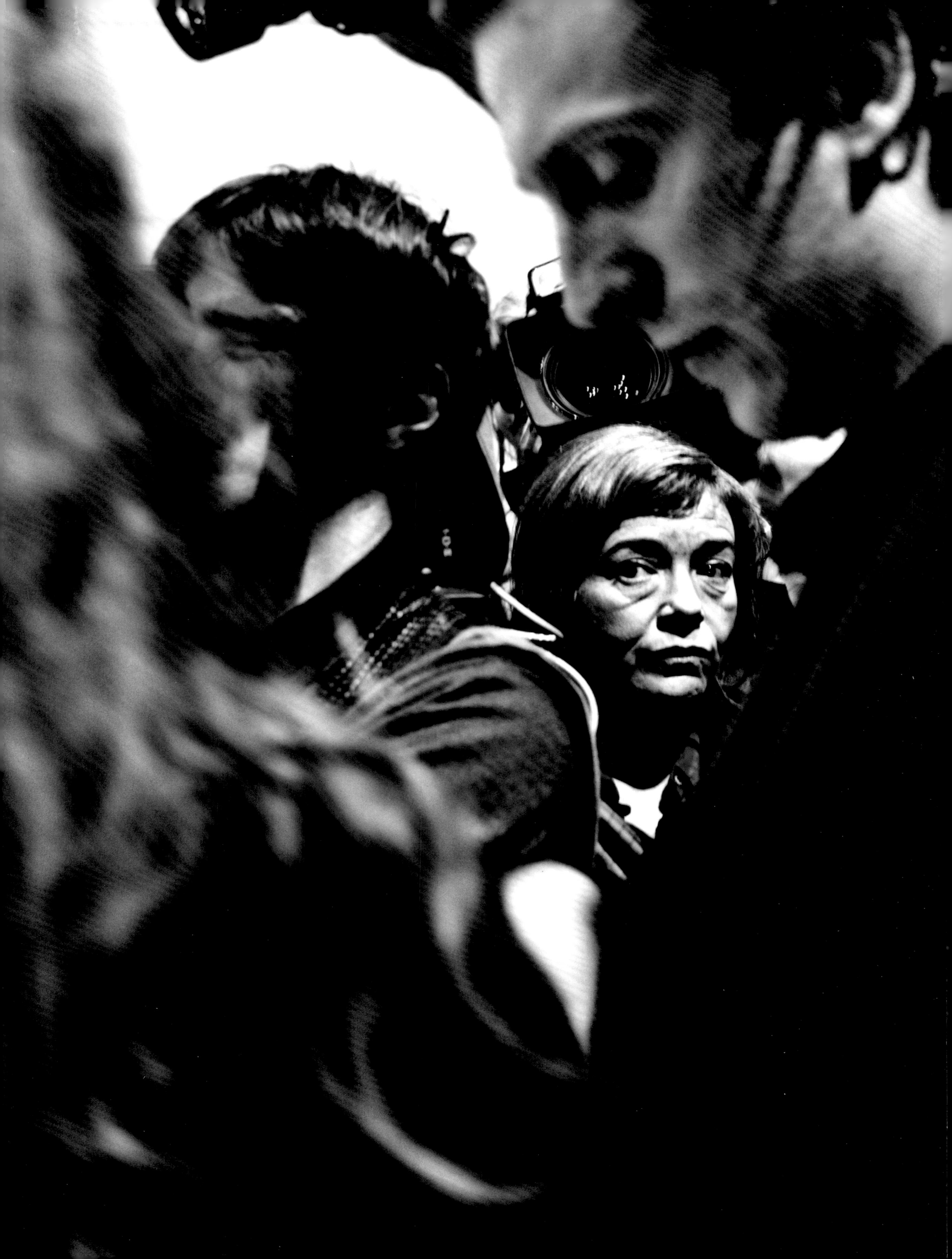

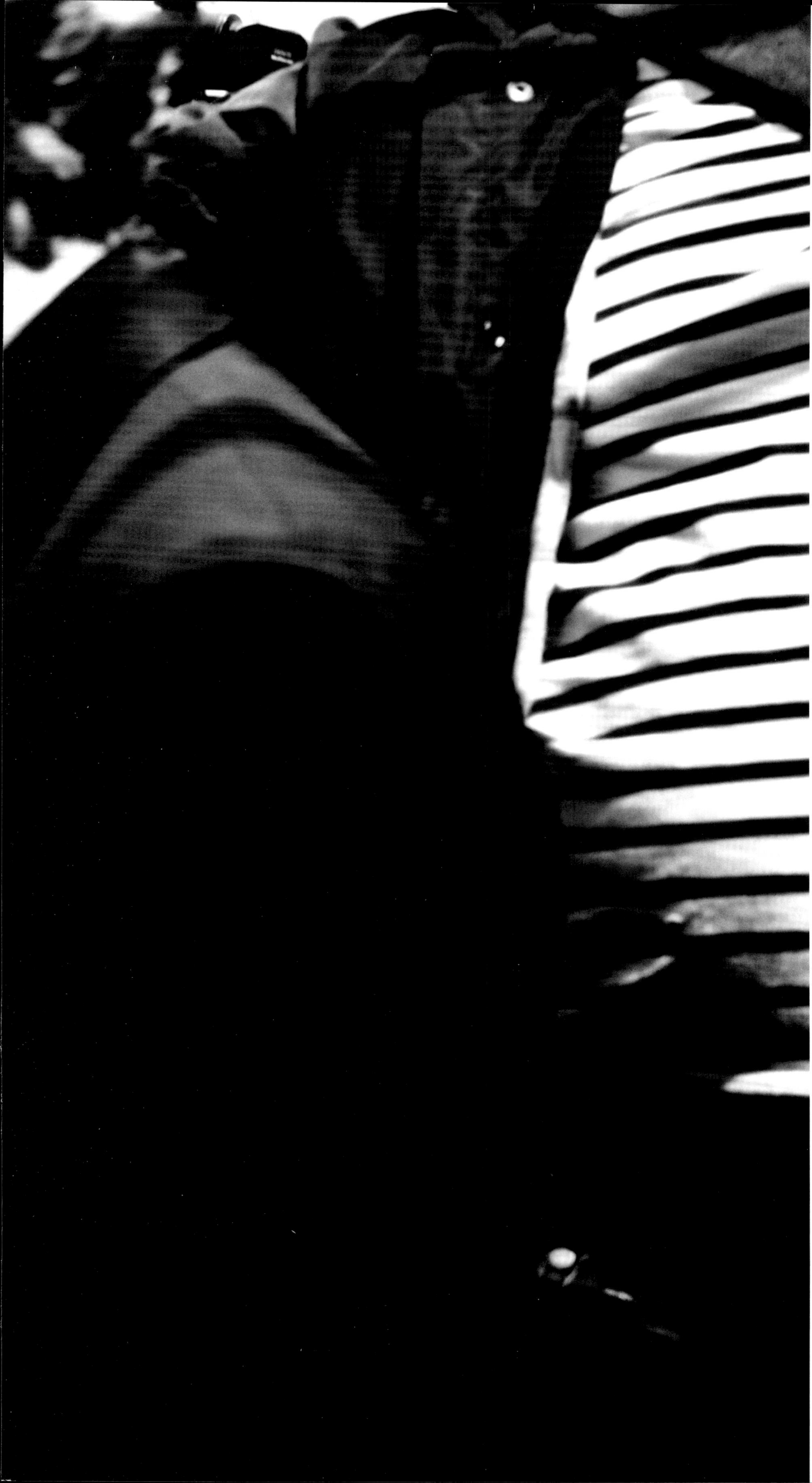

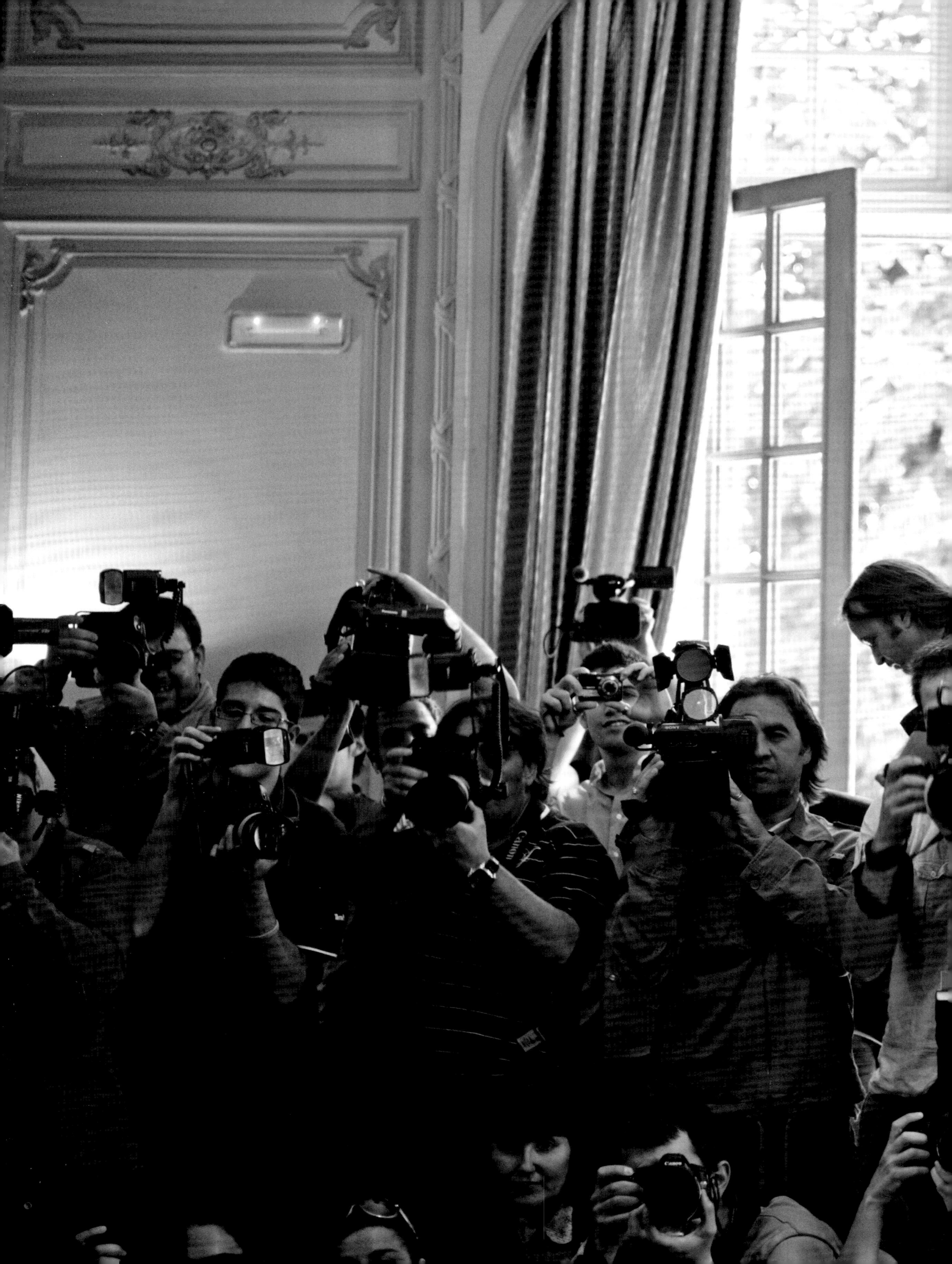

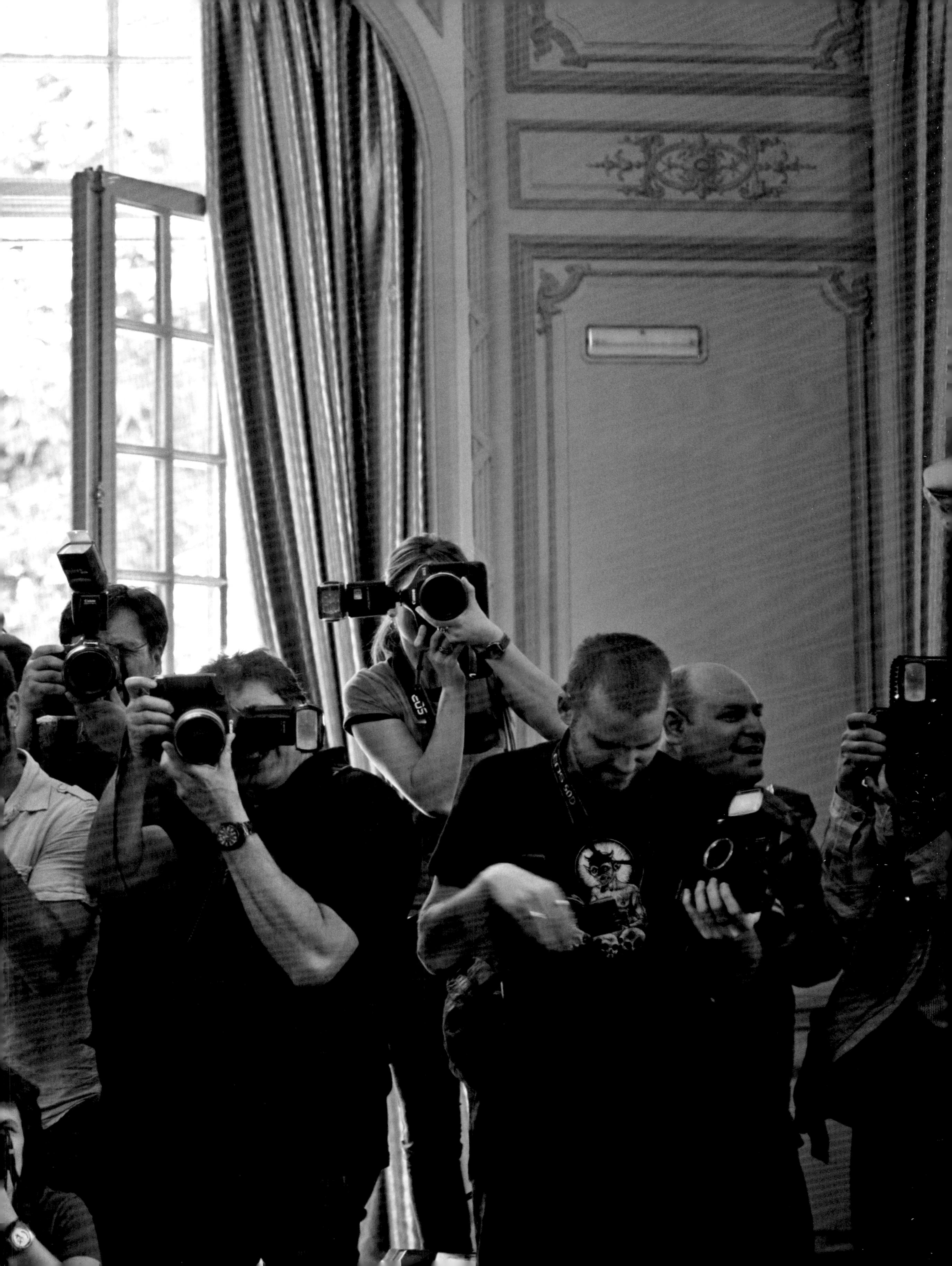

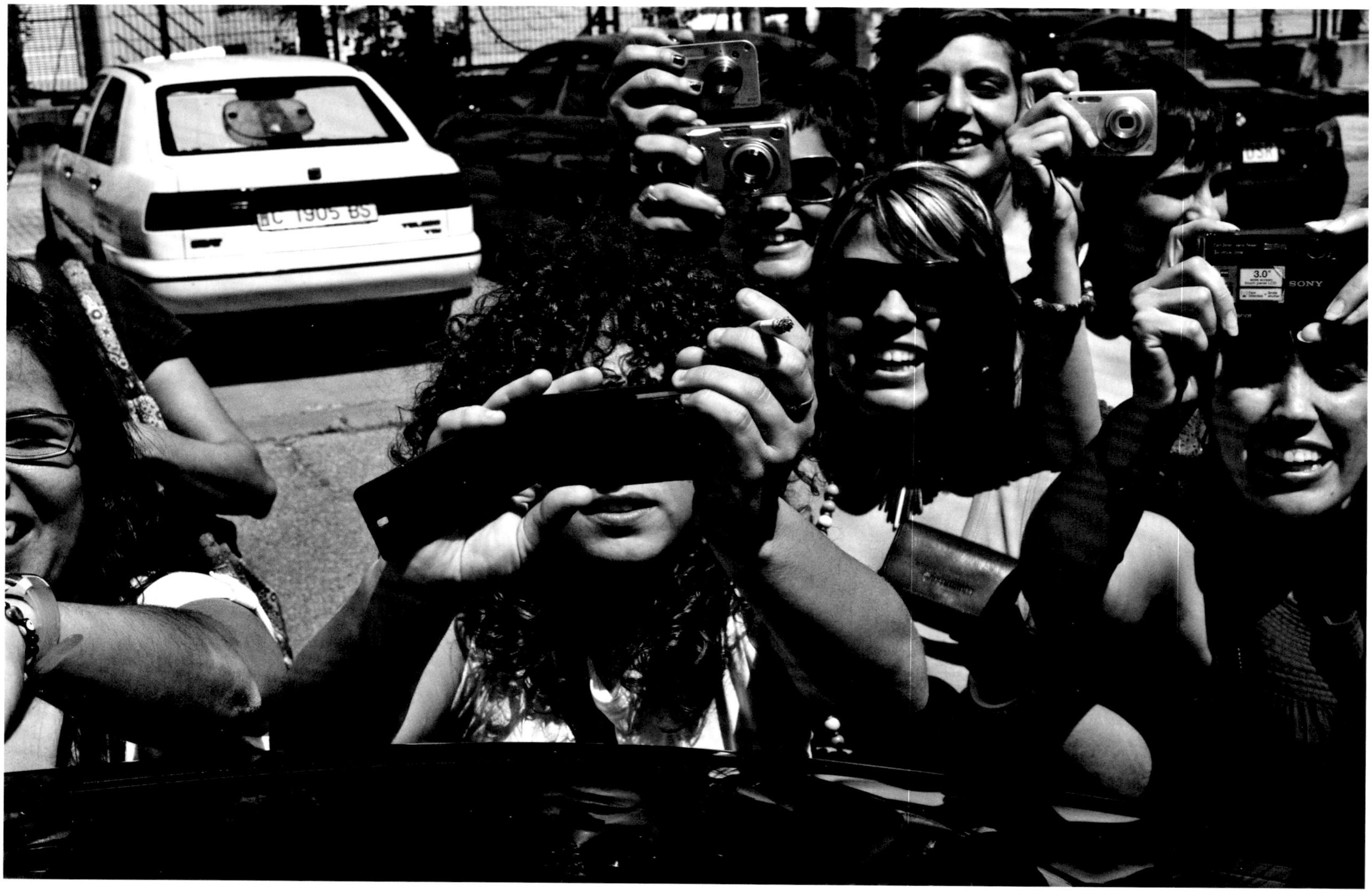
C 1905 BS
SONY

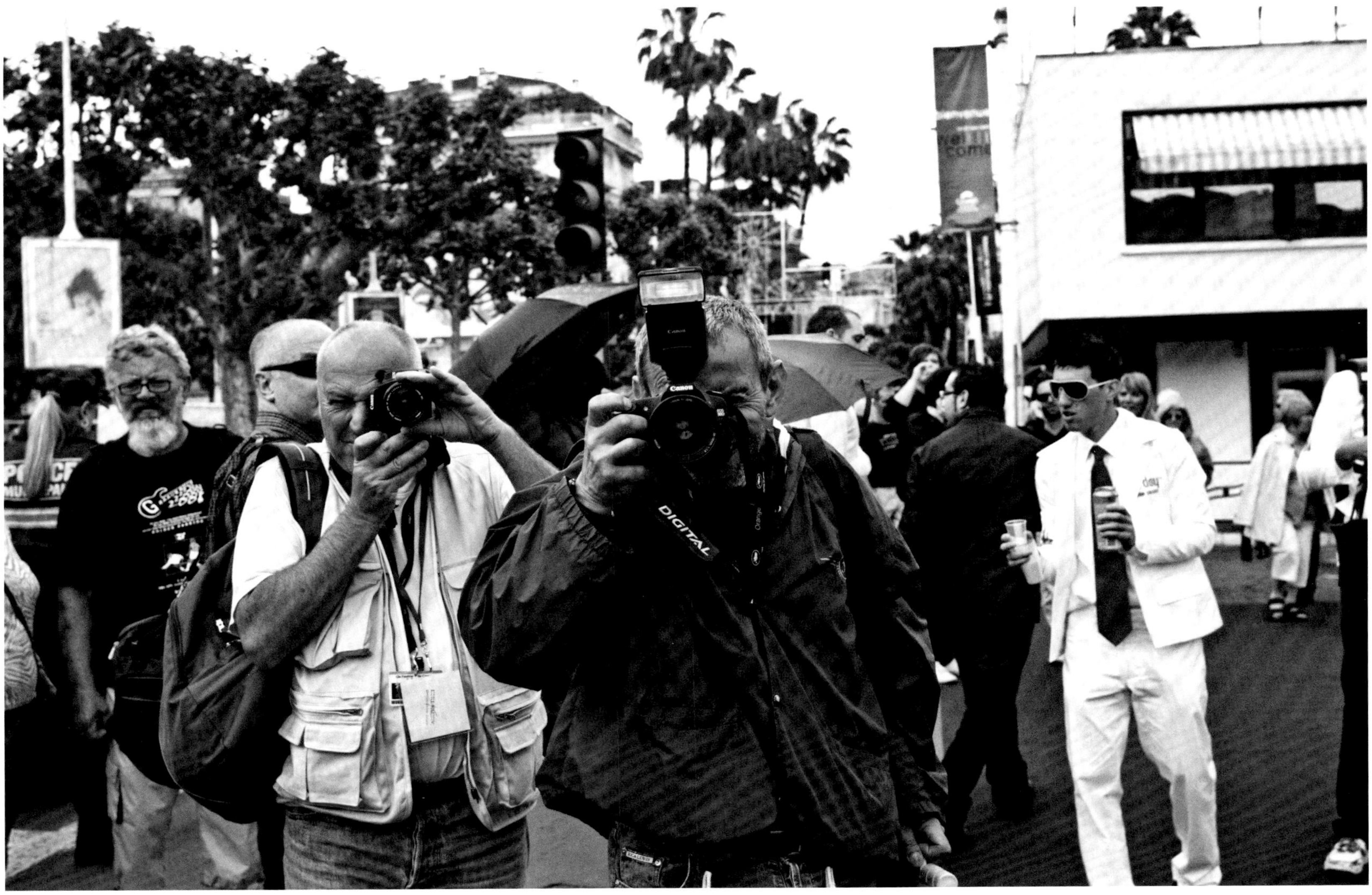
DIGITAL

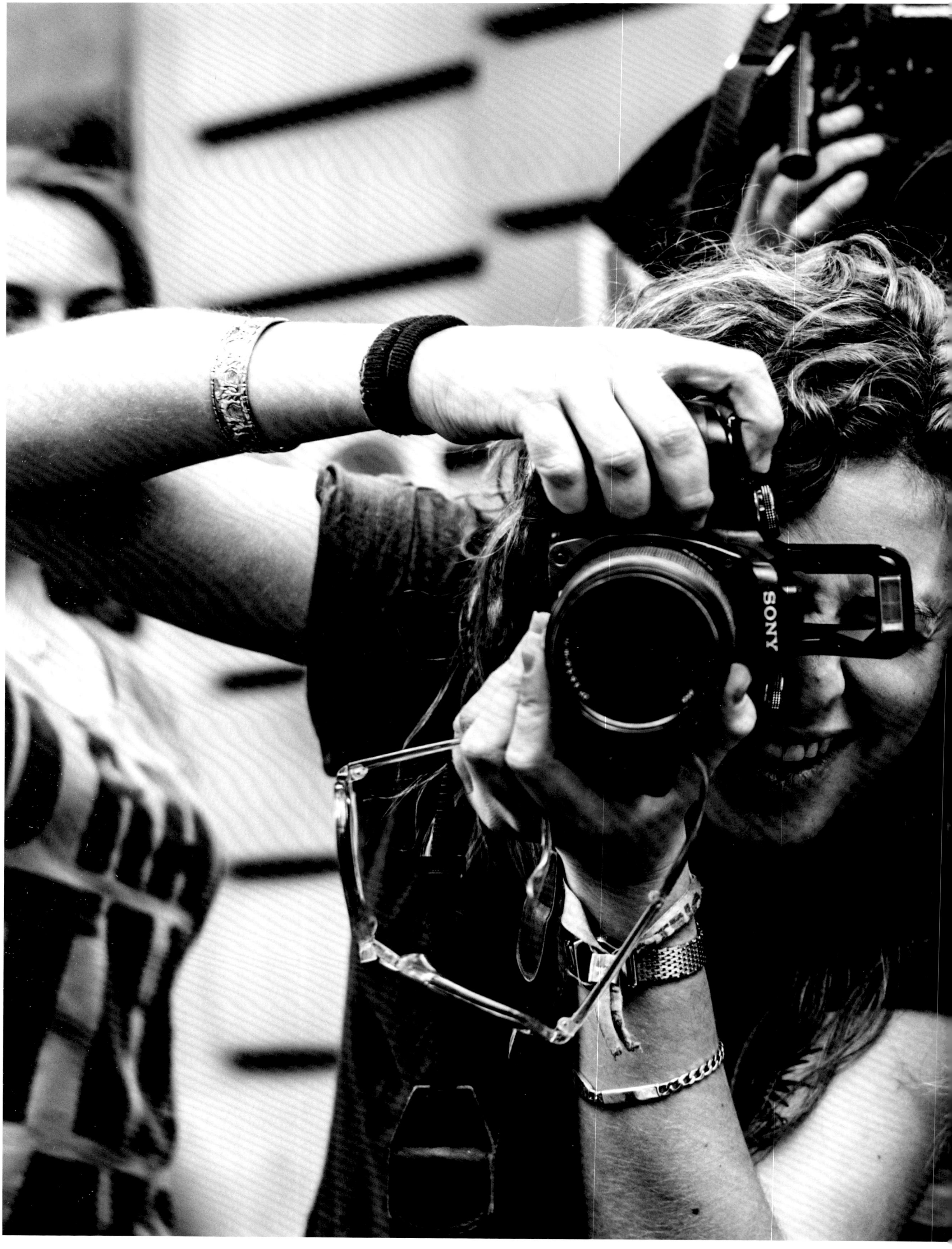
SONY

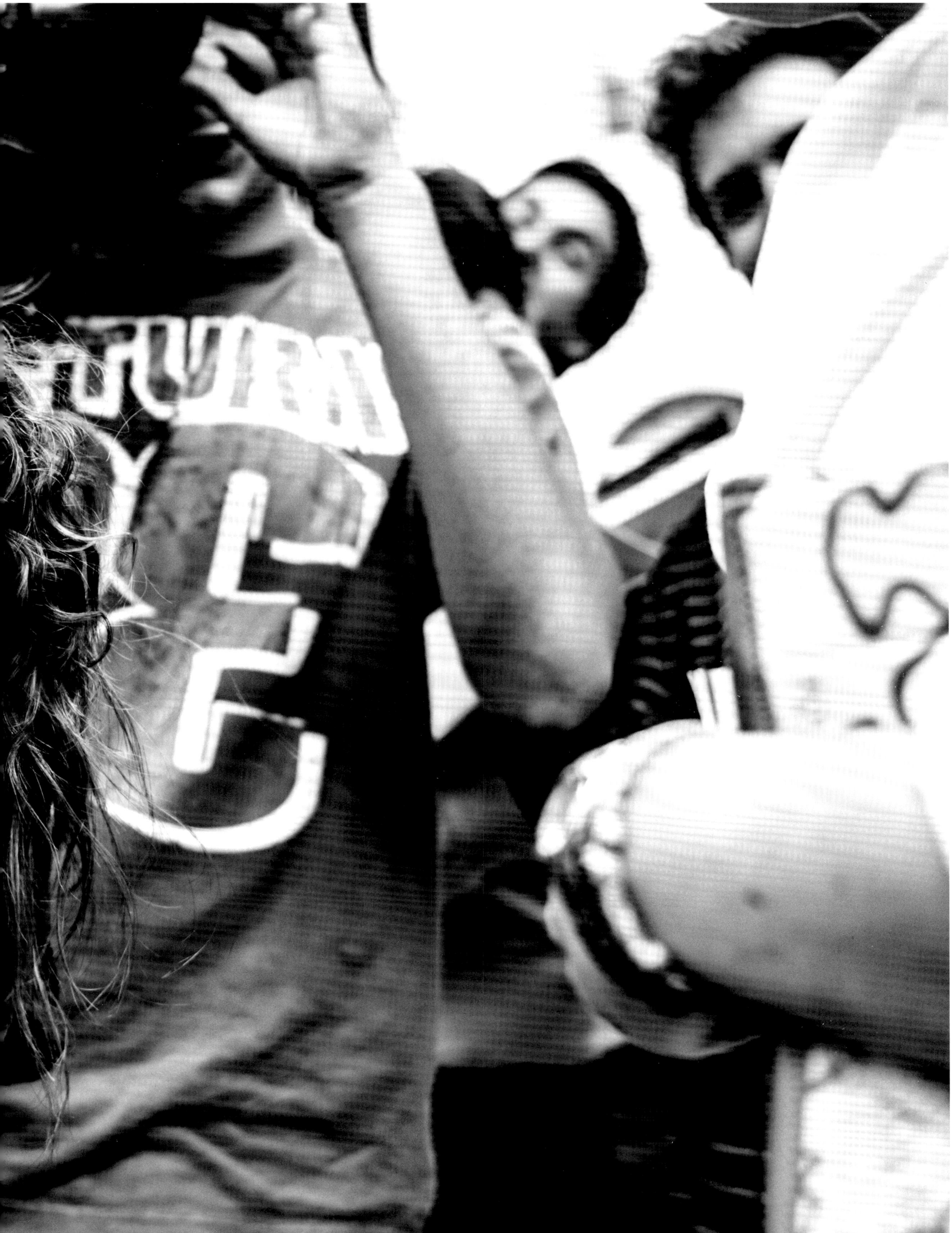

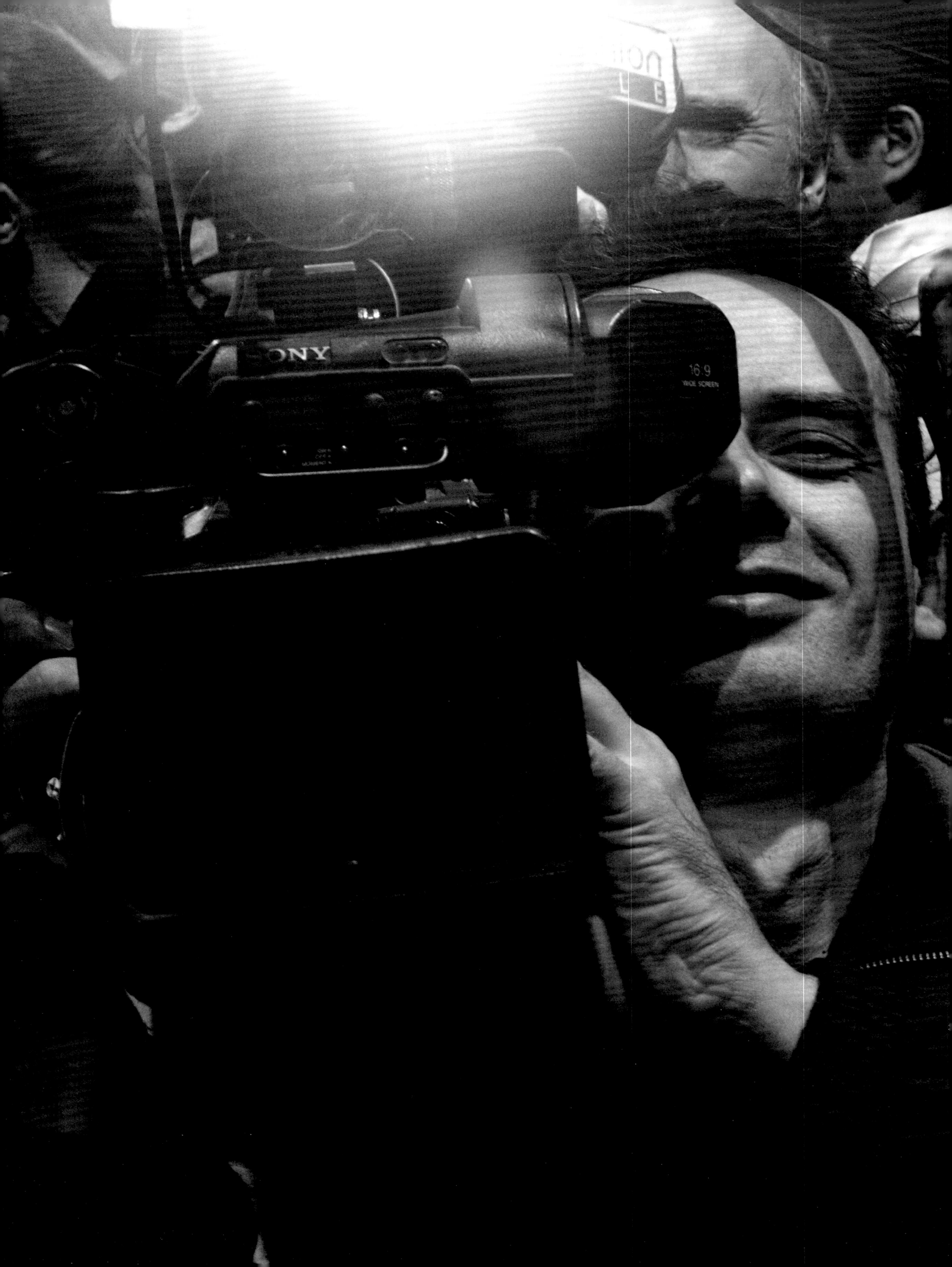
16:9
WIDE SCREEN

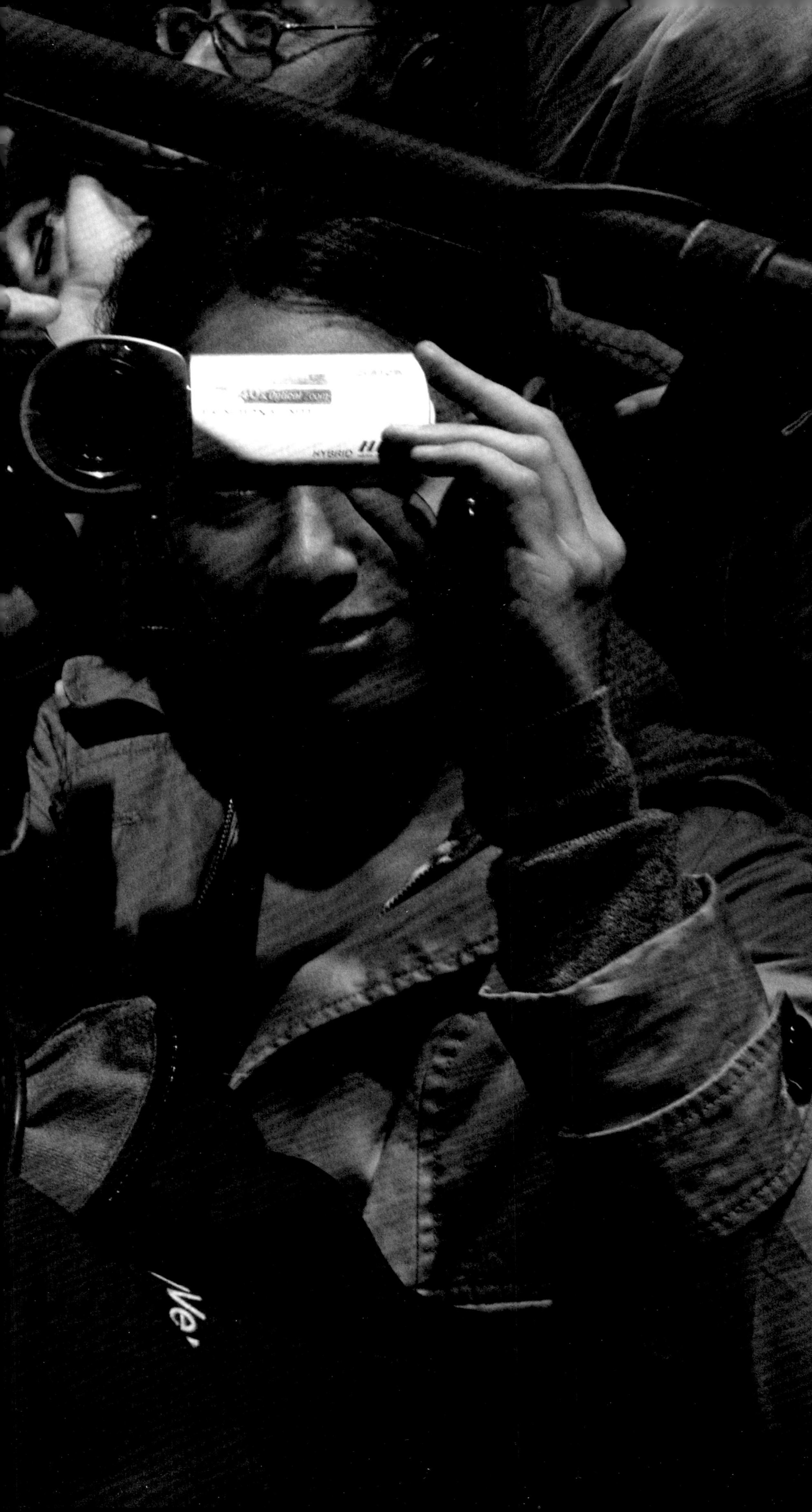
HYBRID

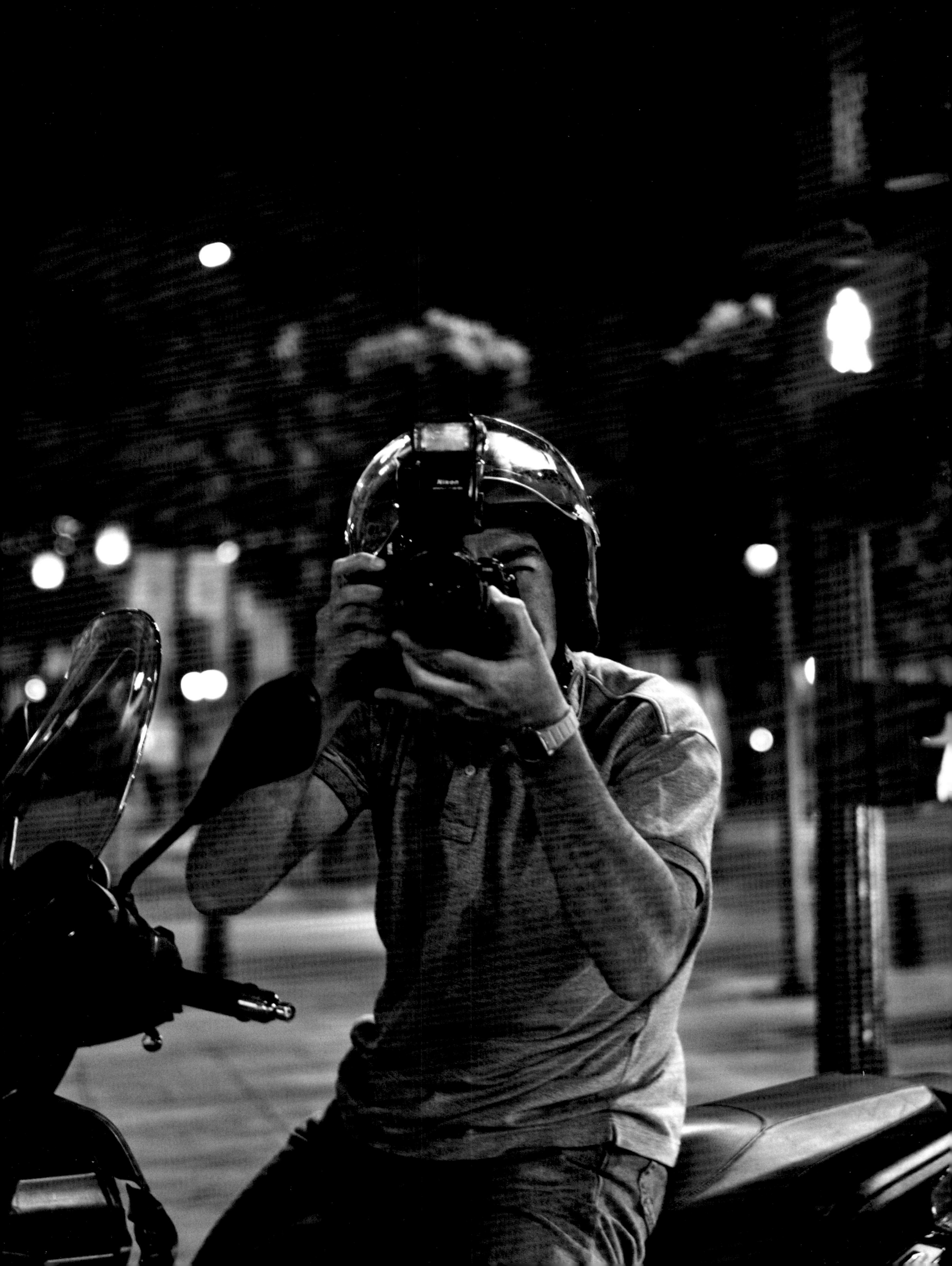

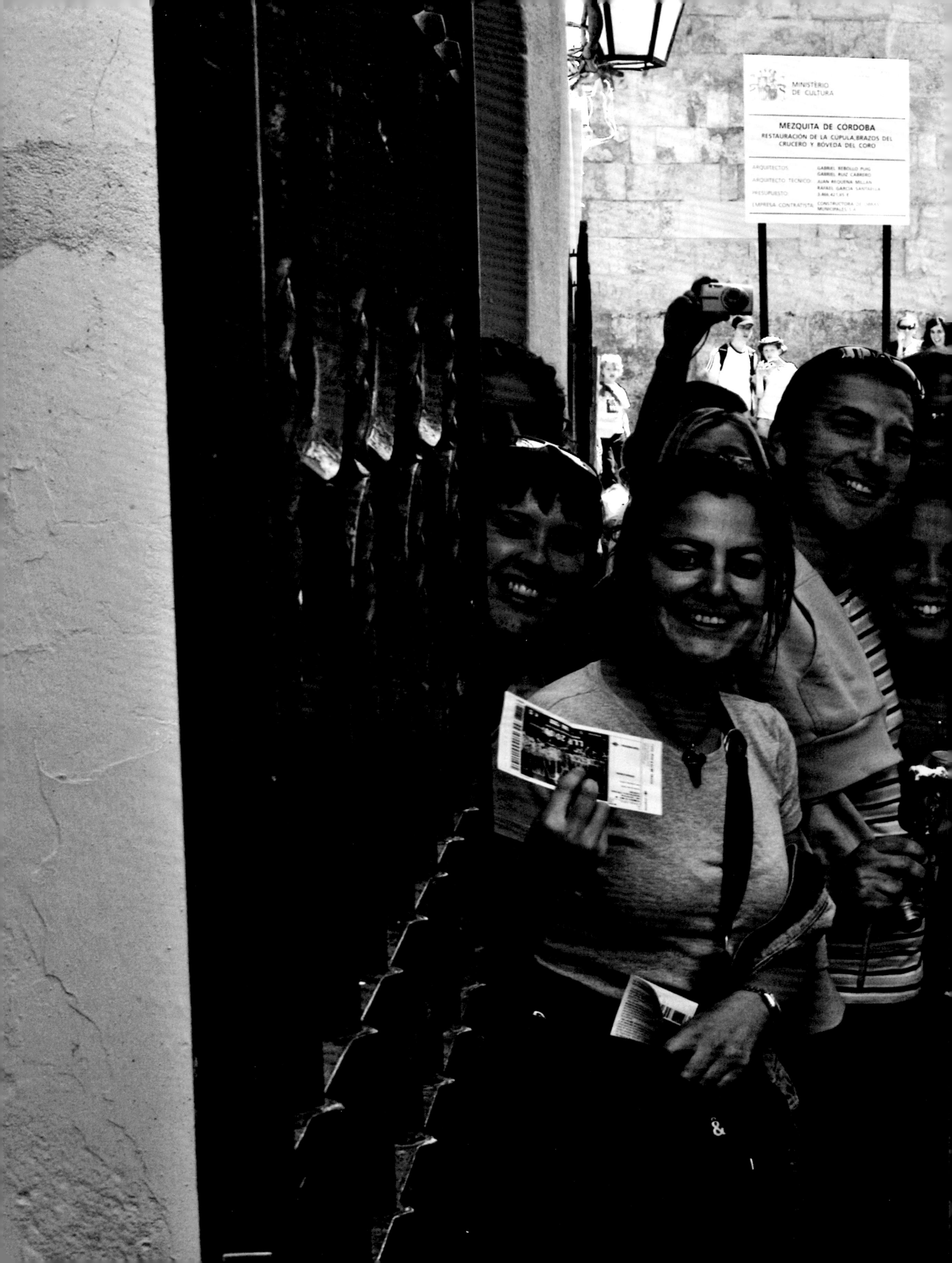
MINISTERIO
DE CULTURA
MEZQUITA DE CORDOBA
RESTAURACIÓN DE LA CUPULA,BRAZOS DEL
CRUCERO Y BÓVEDA DEL CORO
ARQUITECTOS
GABRIEL REBOLLO PUIG
GABRIEL RUIZ CABRERO
ARQUITECTO TECNICO
JUAN REQUENA MILLAN
RAFAEL GARCIA SANTAELLA
PRESUPUESTO
EMPRESA CONTRATISTA

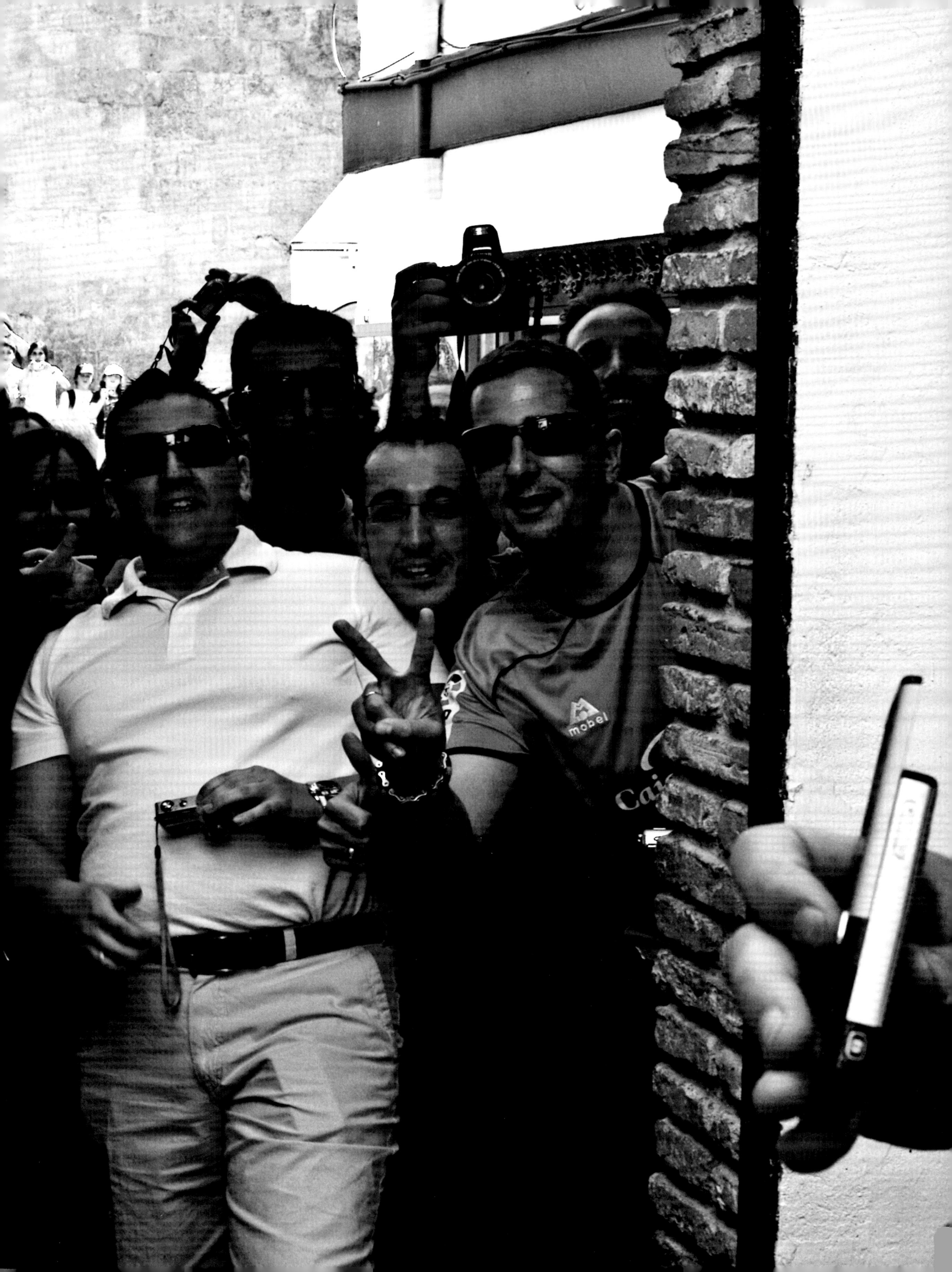
mobel

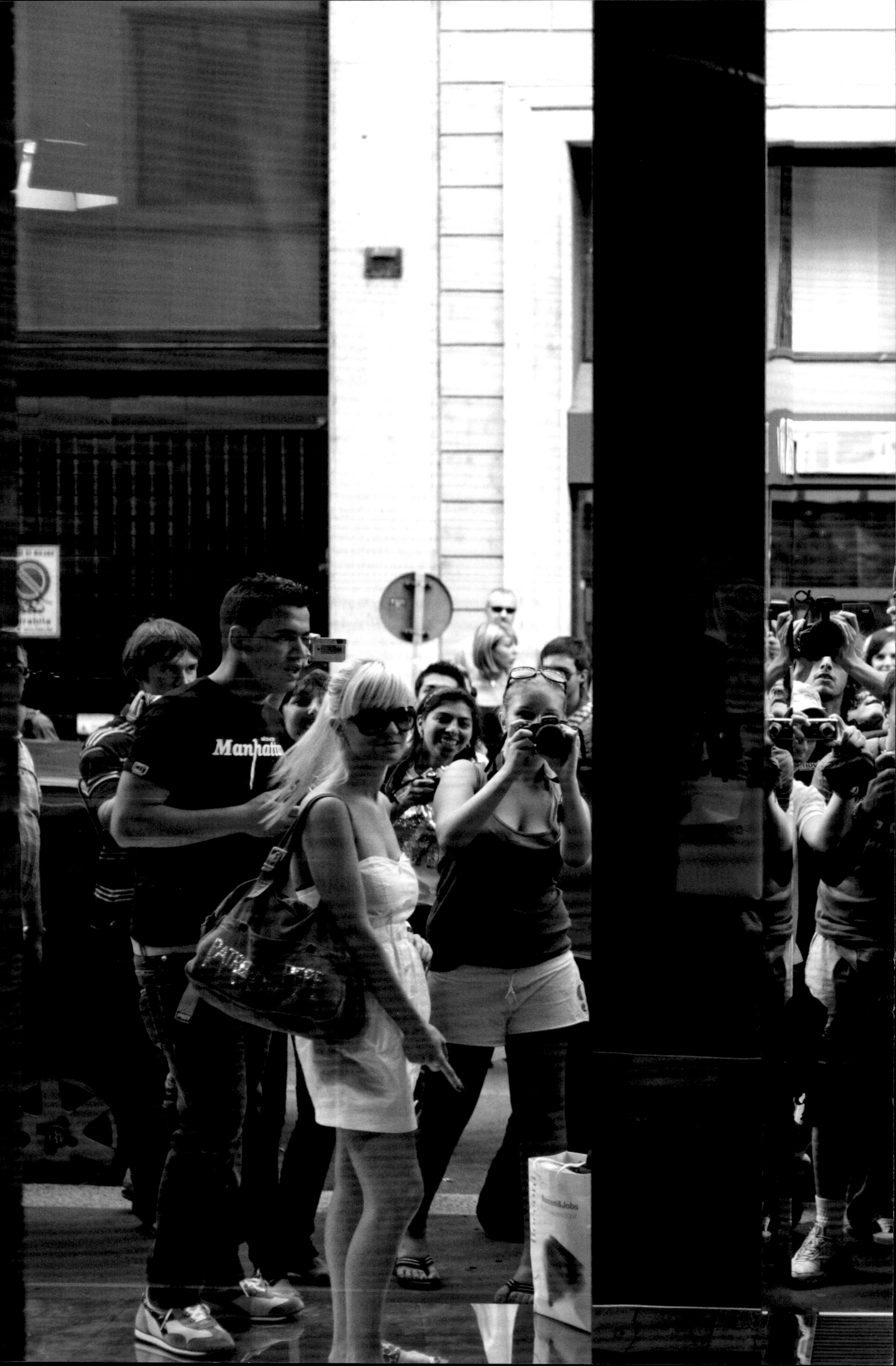

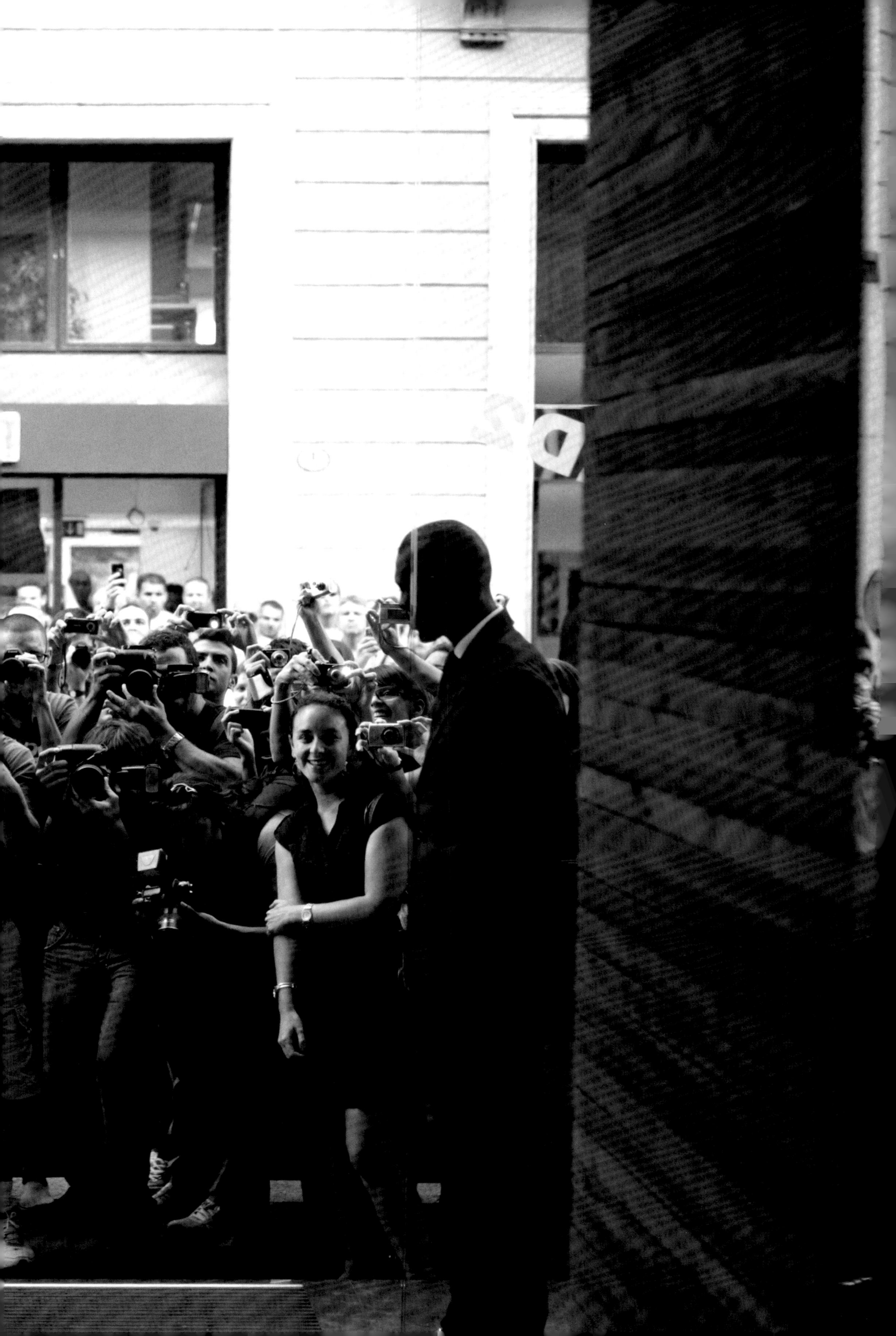

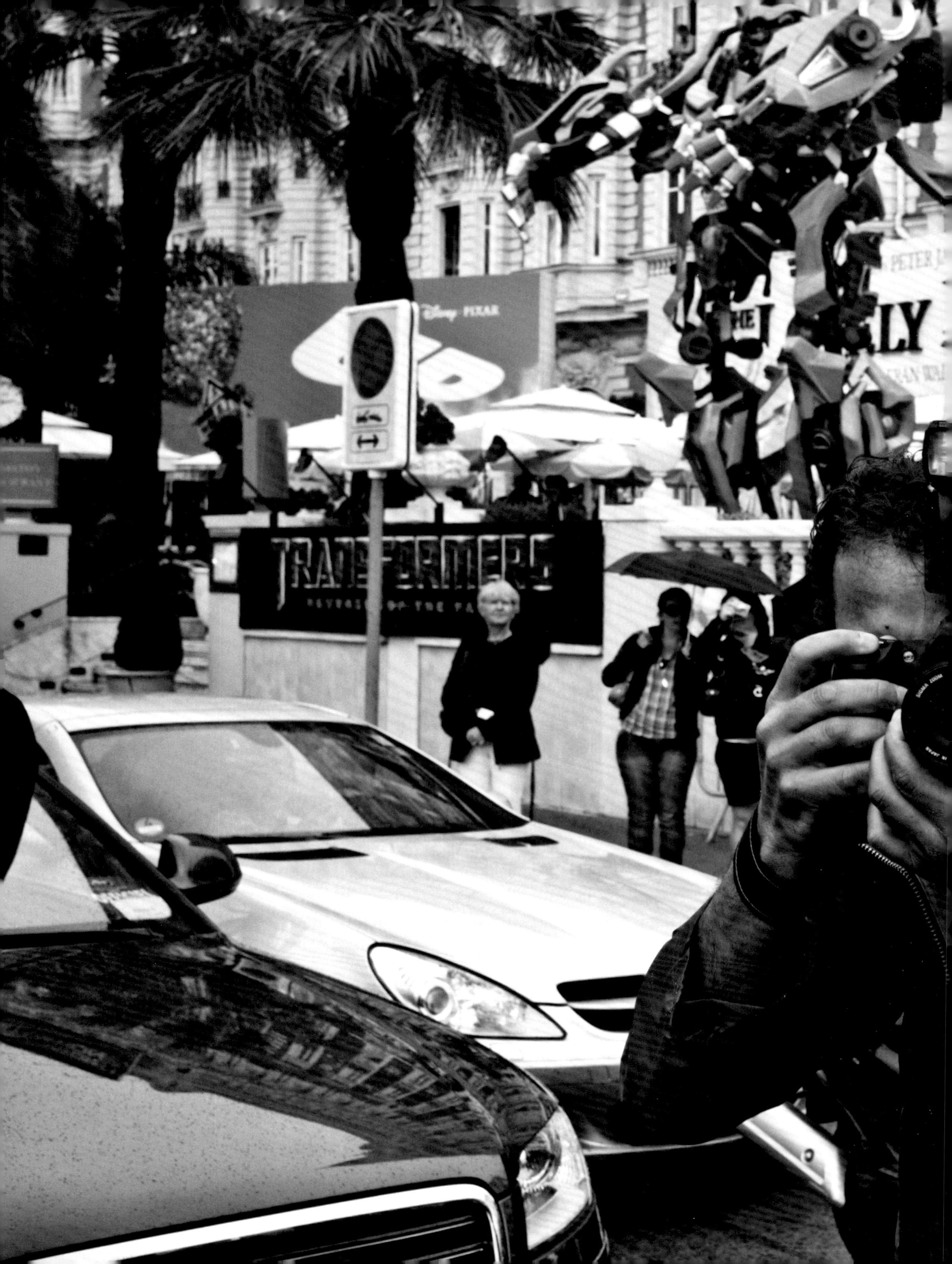
Disney · PIXAR

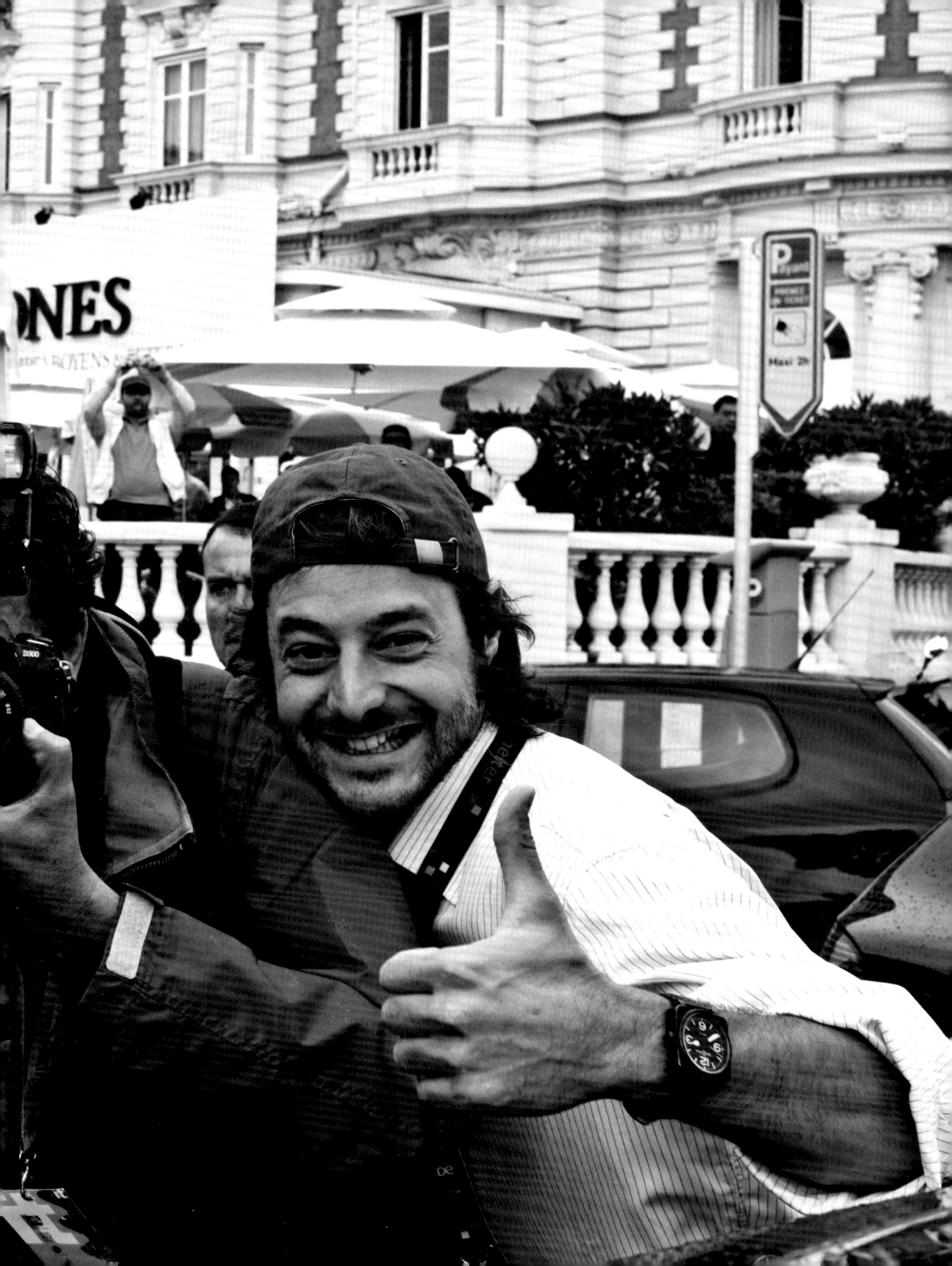
ONES
D300

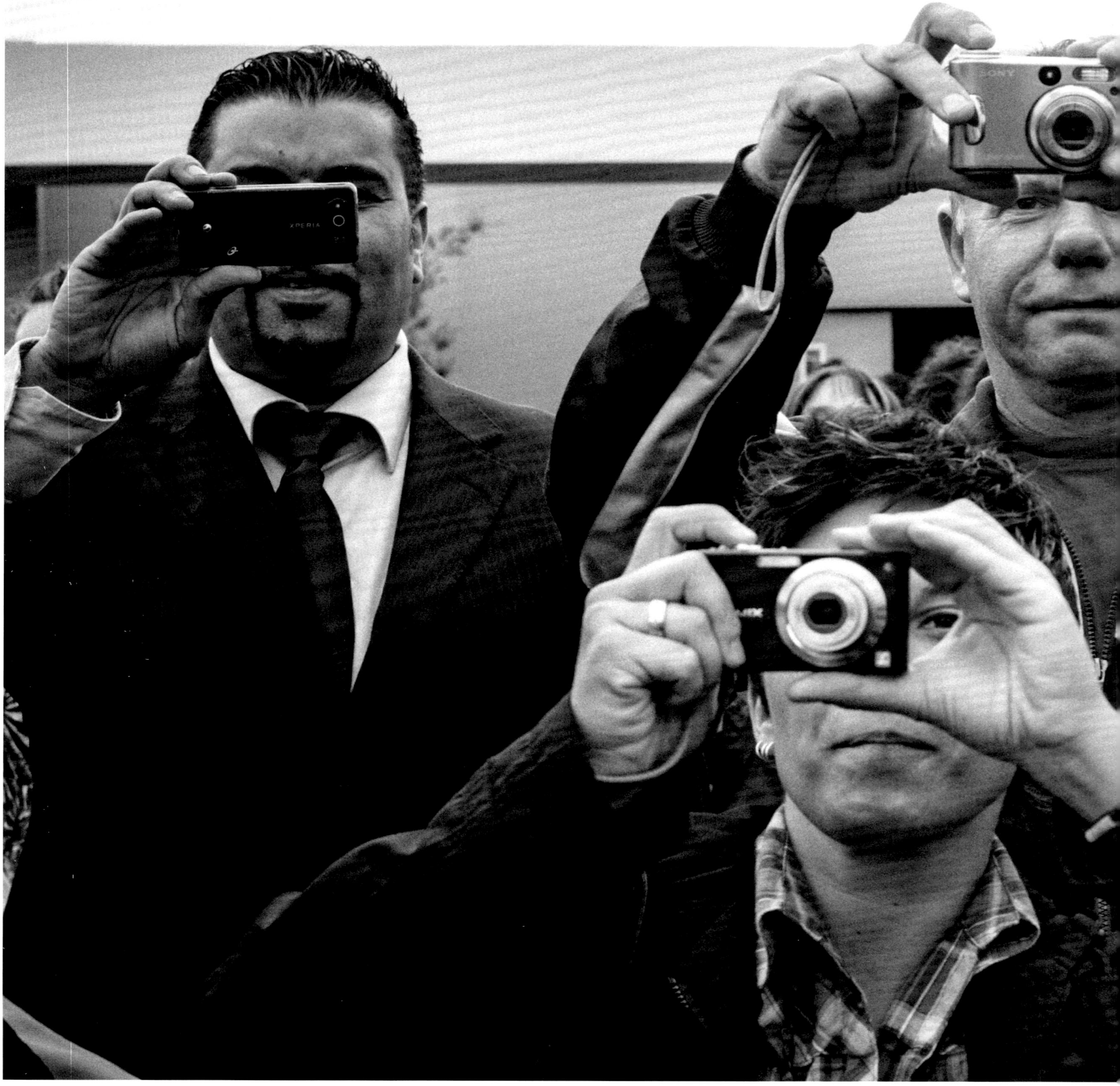
XPERIA
SONY

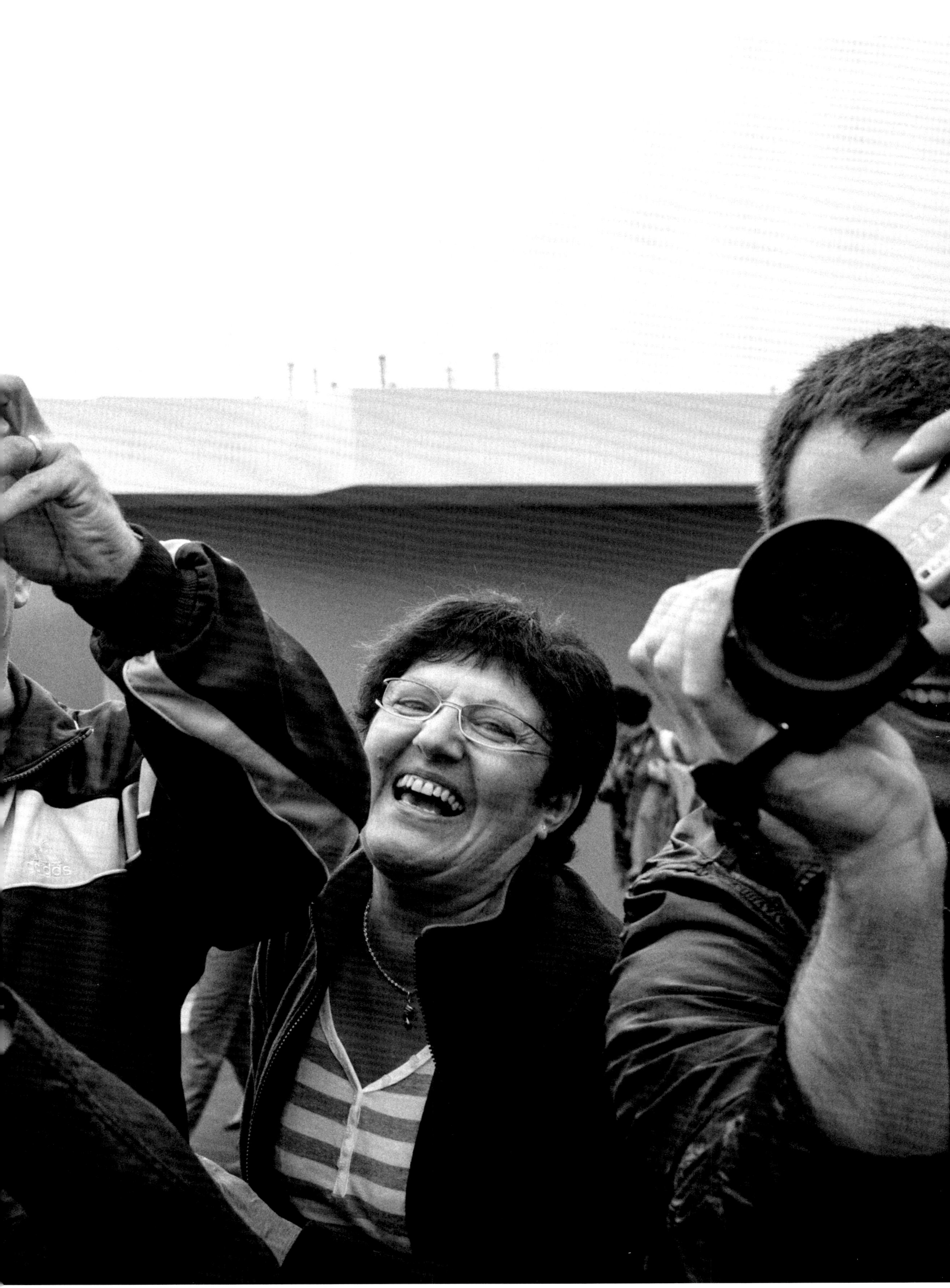

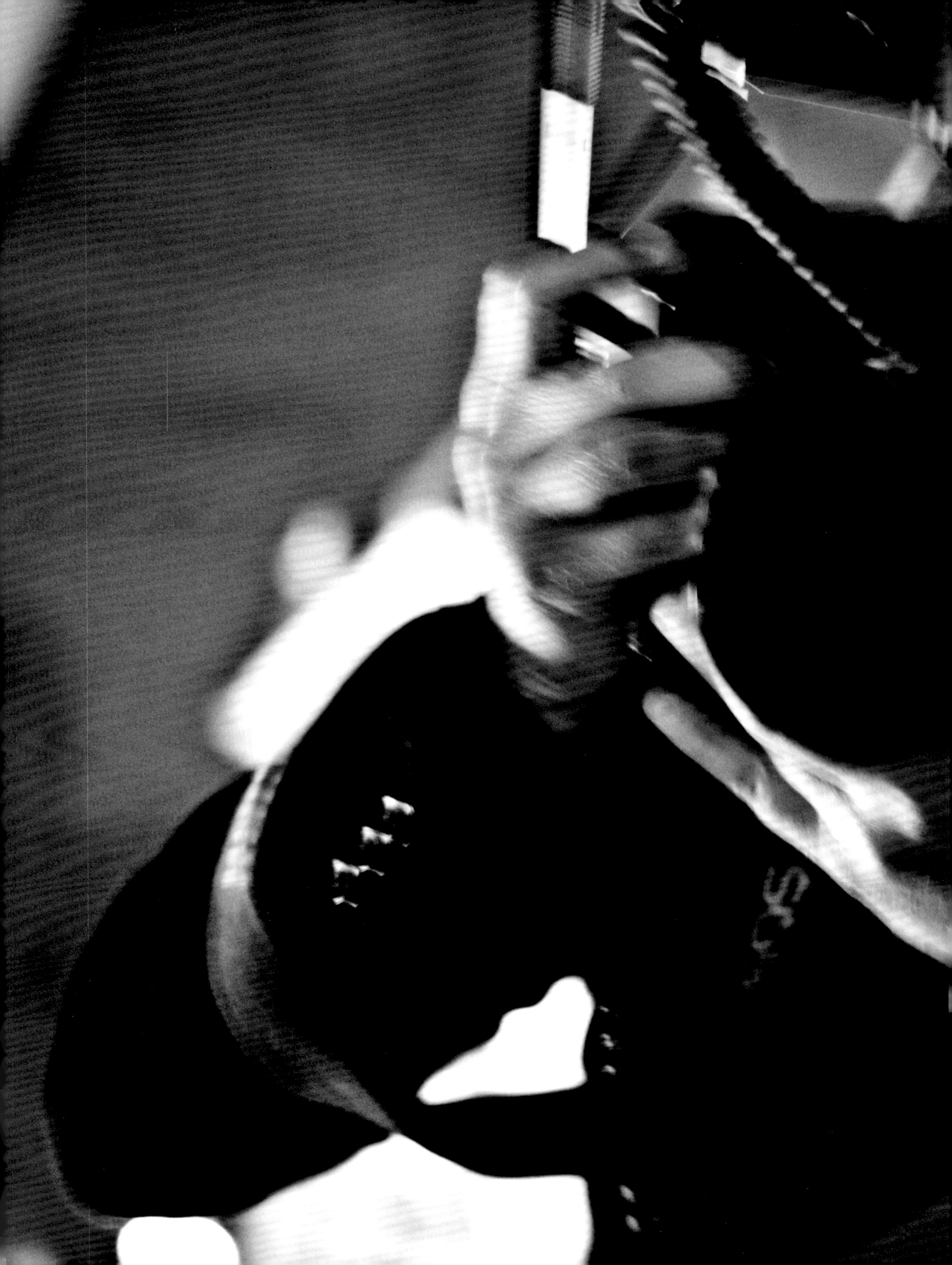

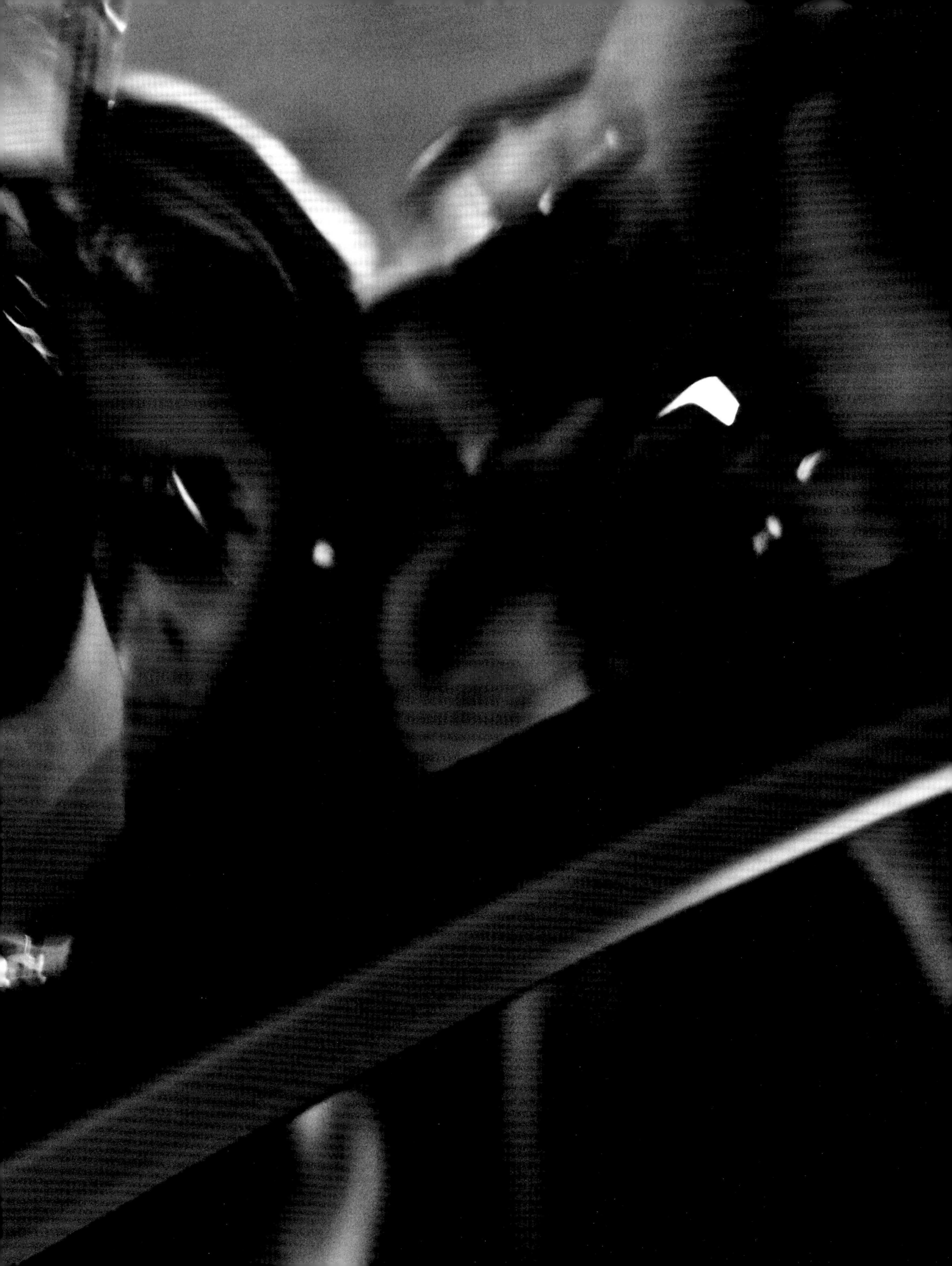

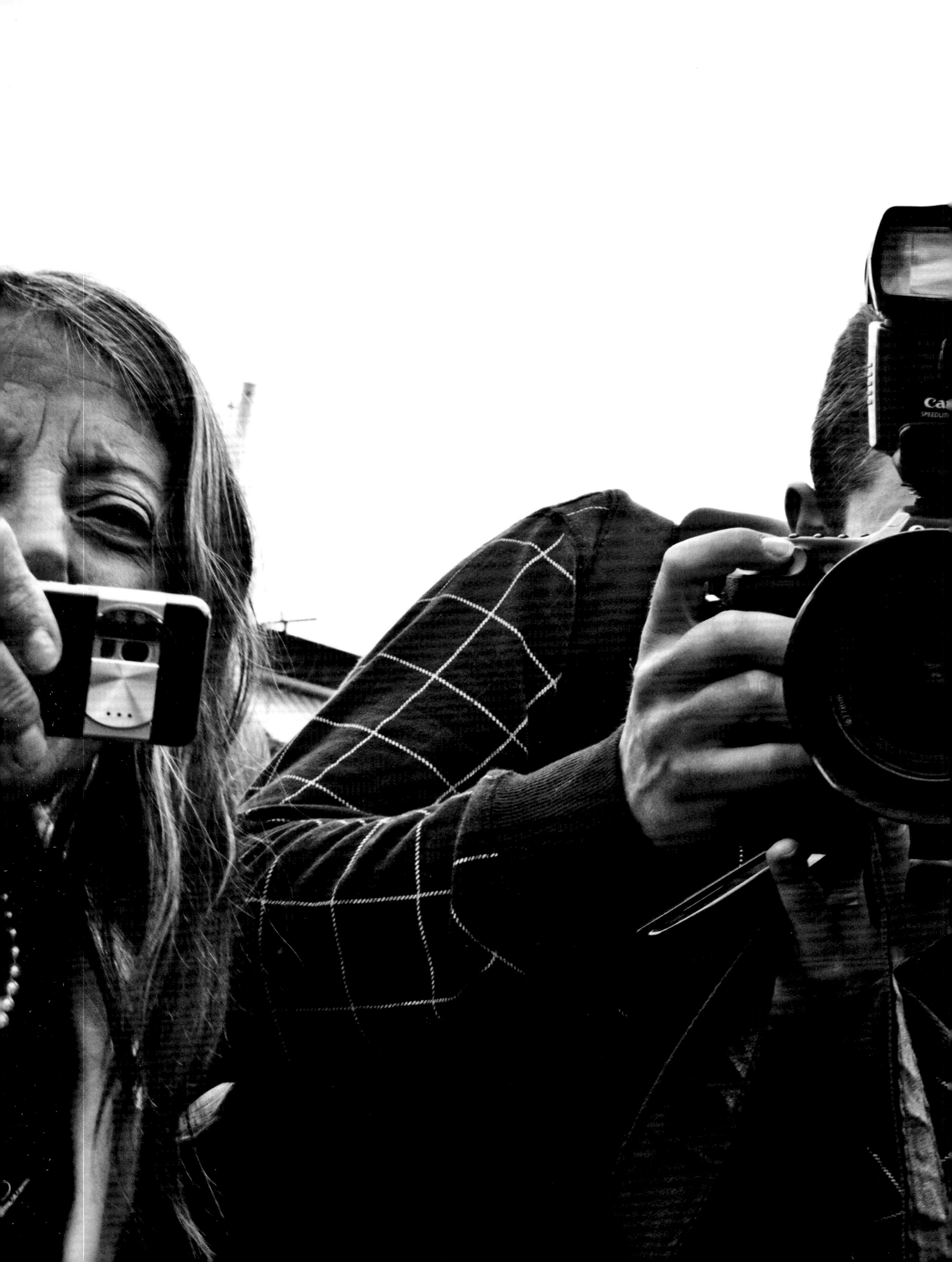

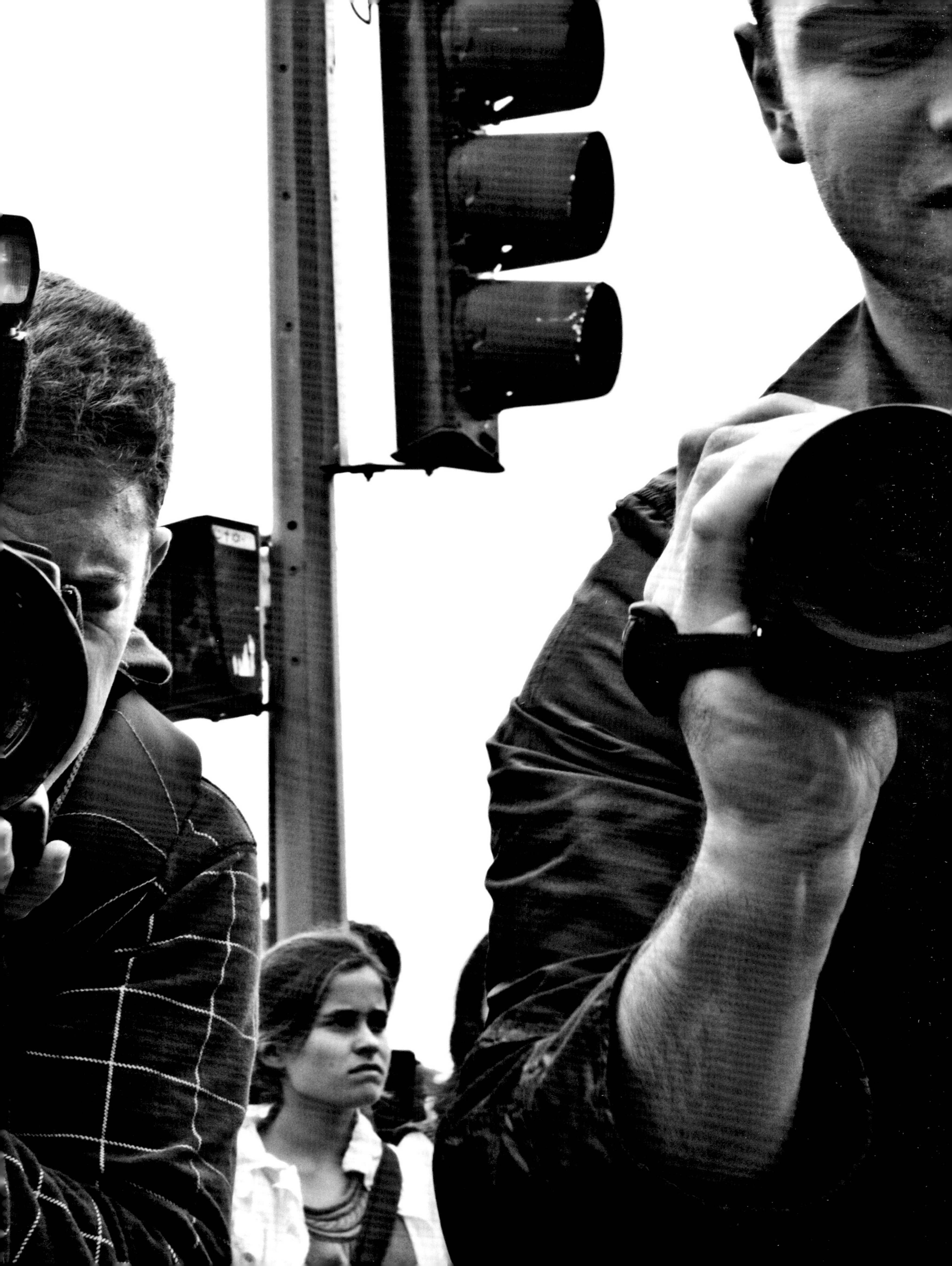

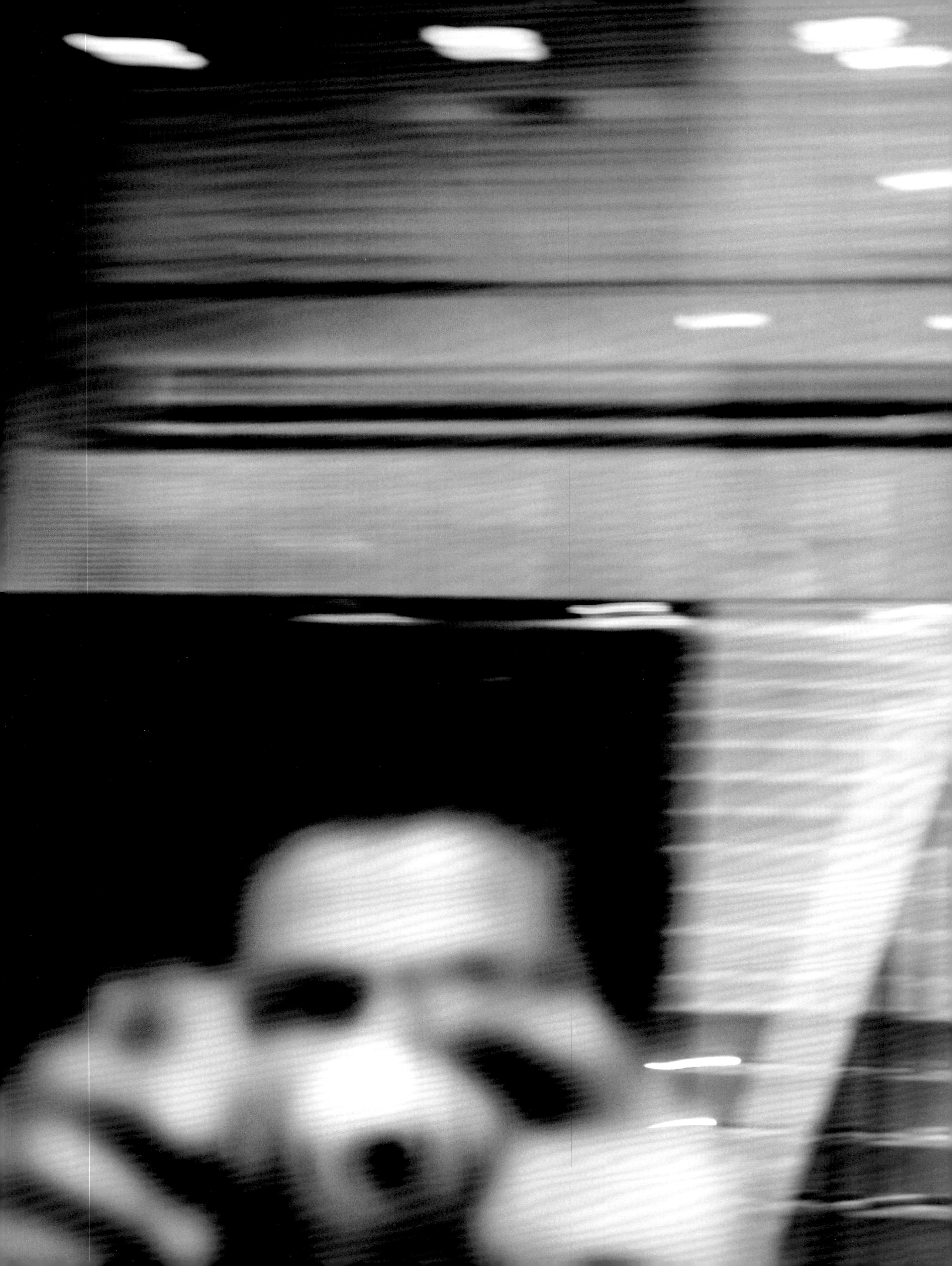

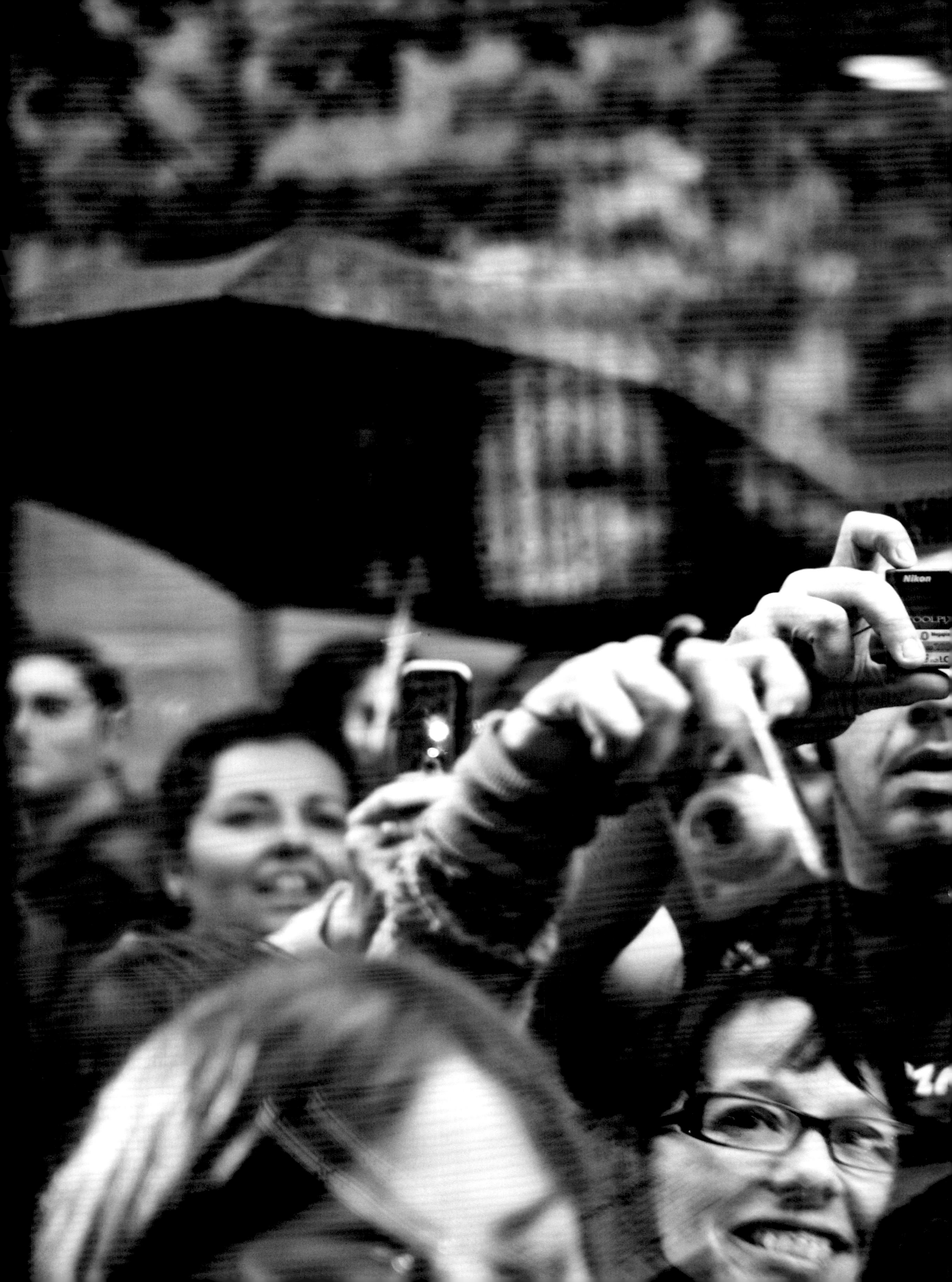
Nikon

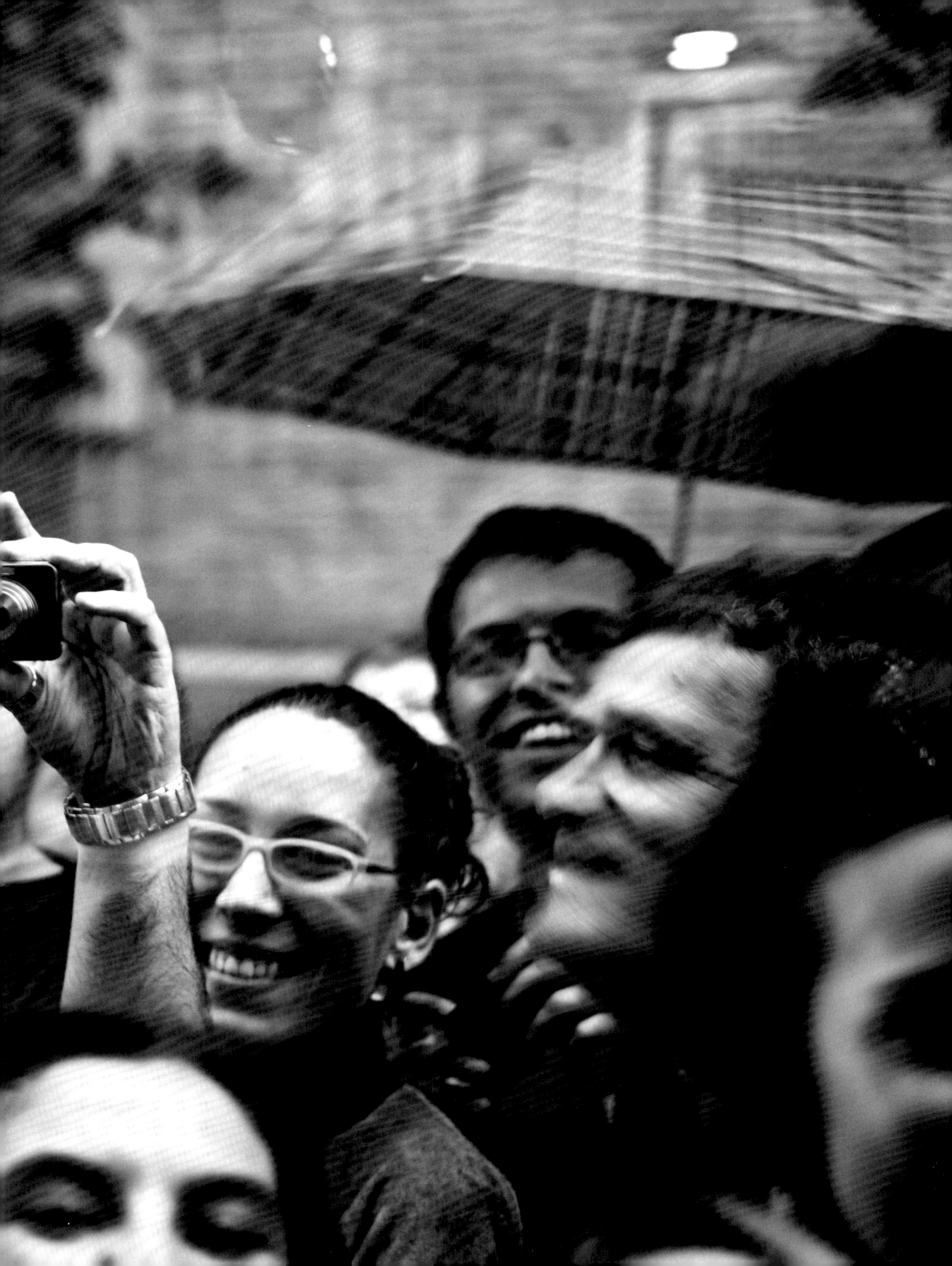

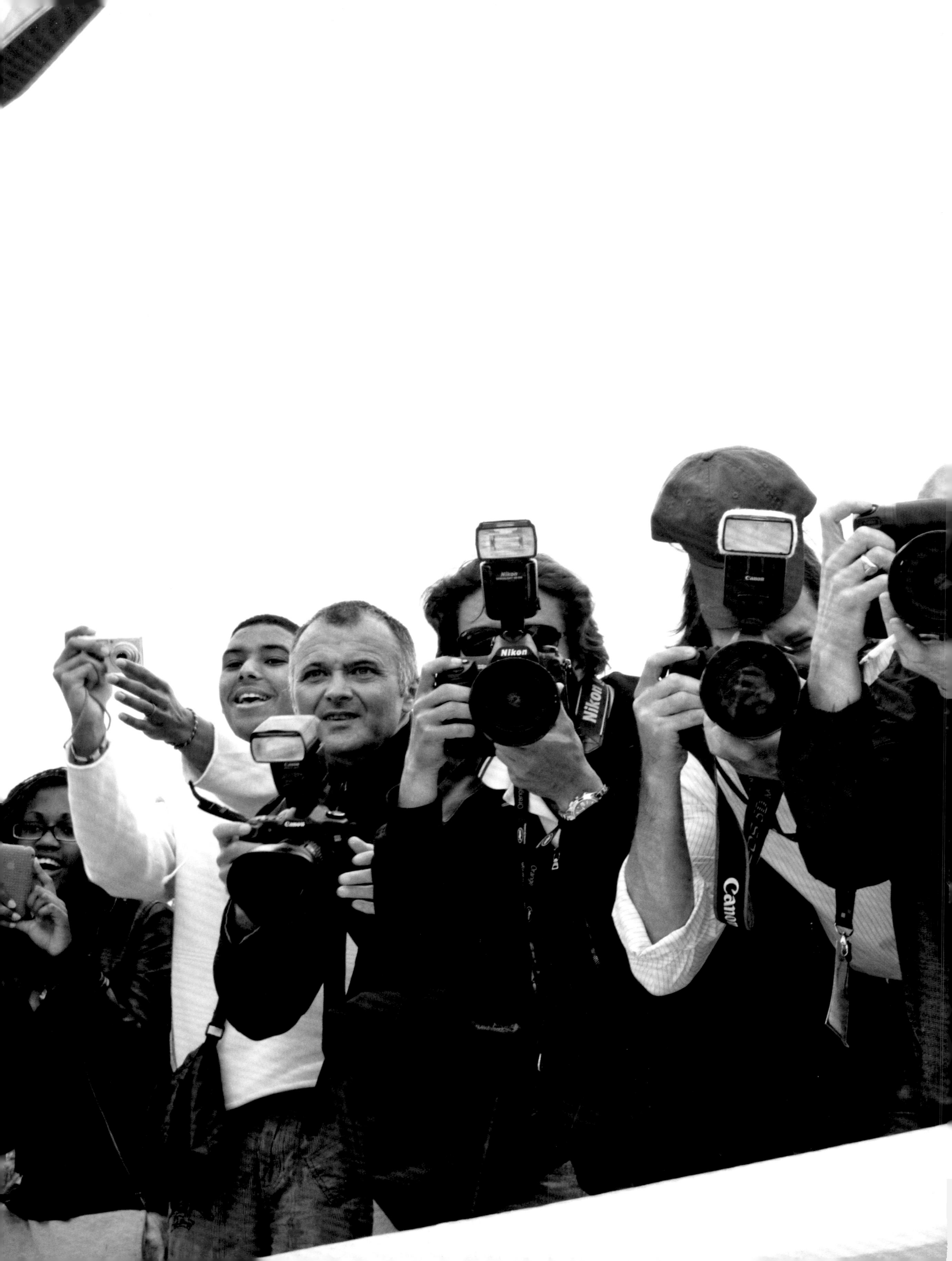
Nikon
Nikon
Nikon
Canon

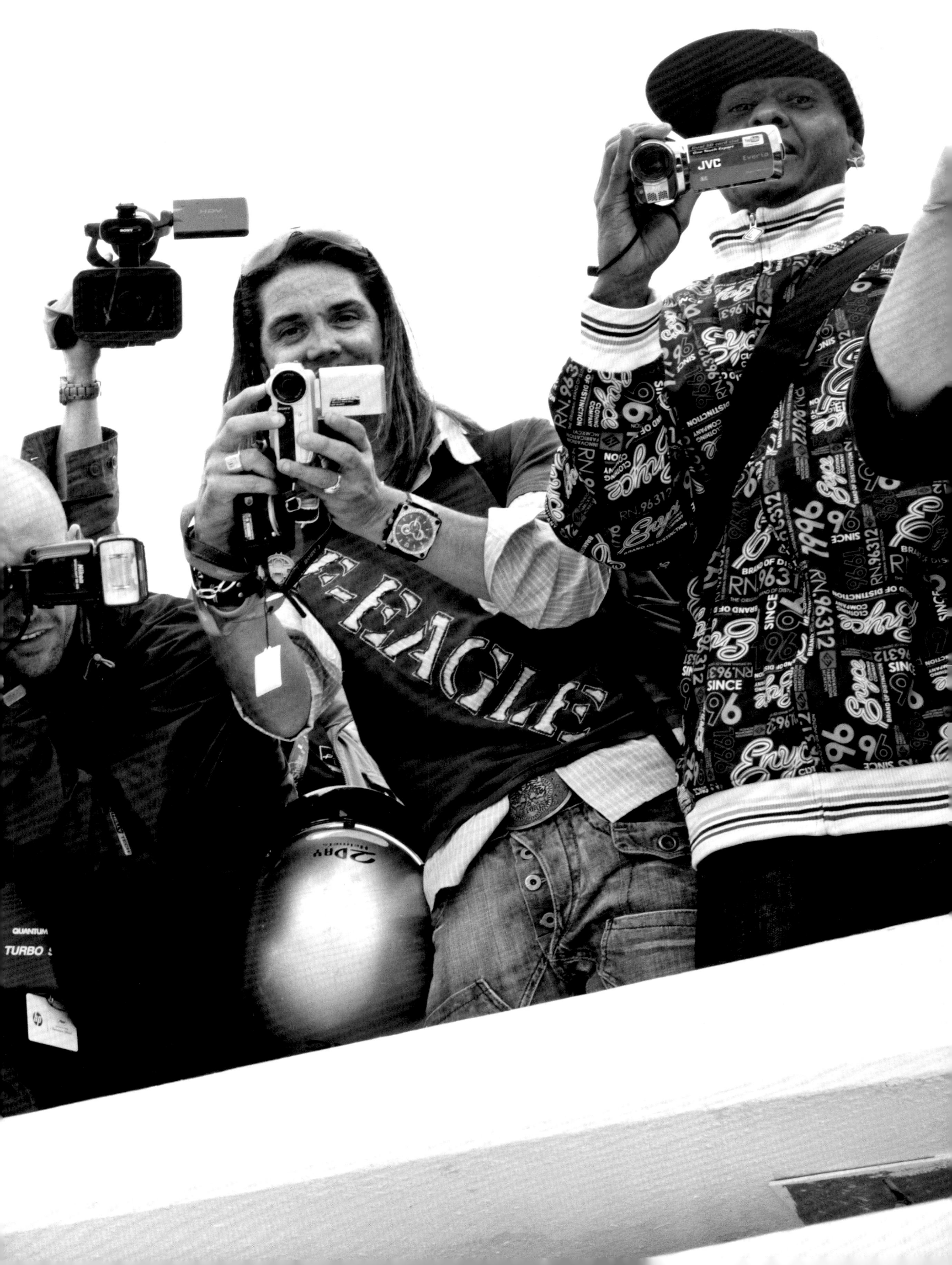
JVC
EAGLE
SINCE
1996
RN.96312
BRAND OF DISTINCTION
QUANTUM
TURBO

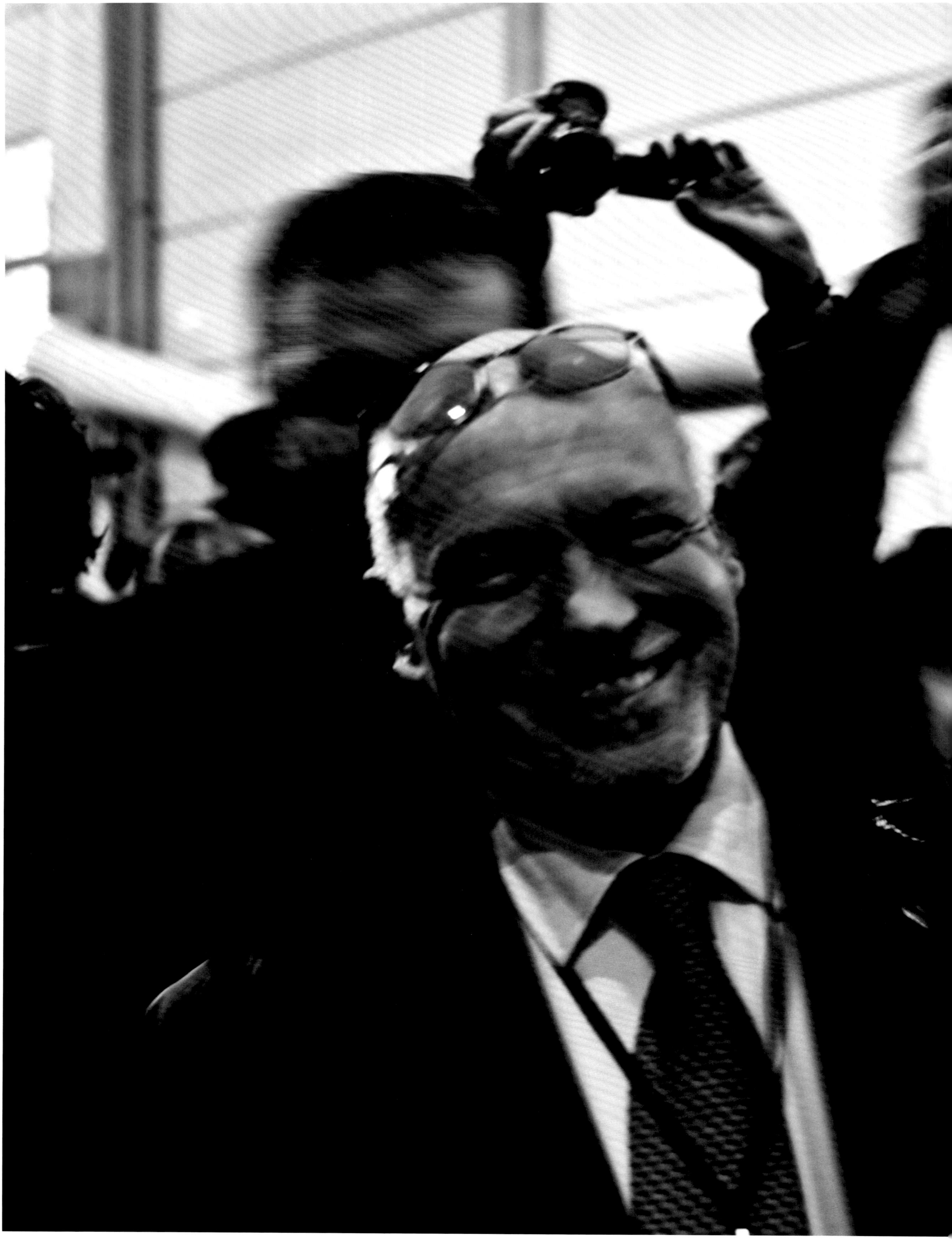

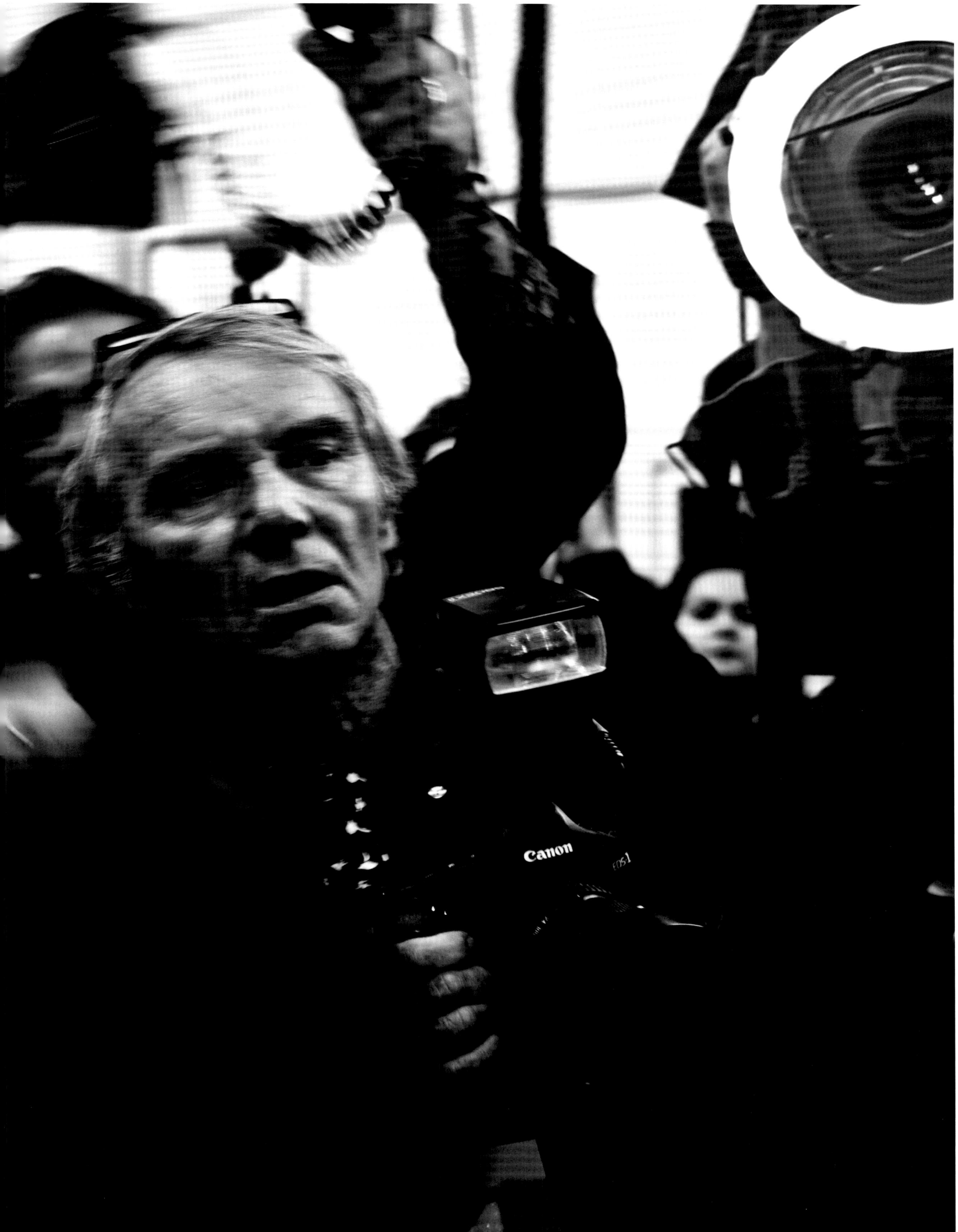
Canon

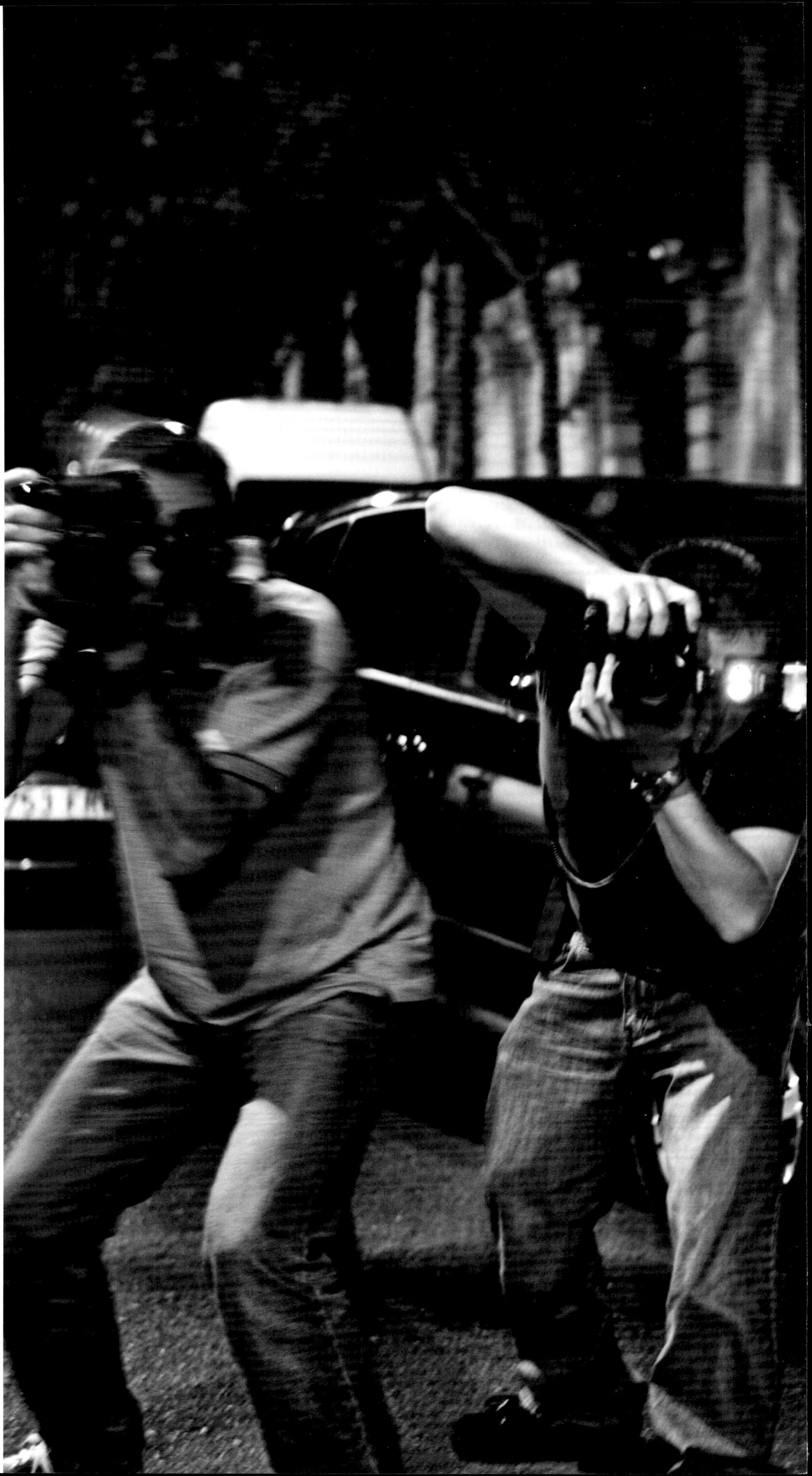

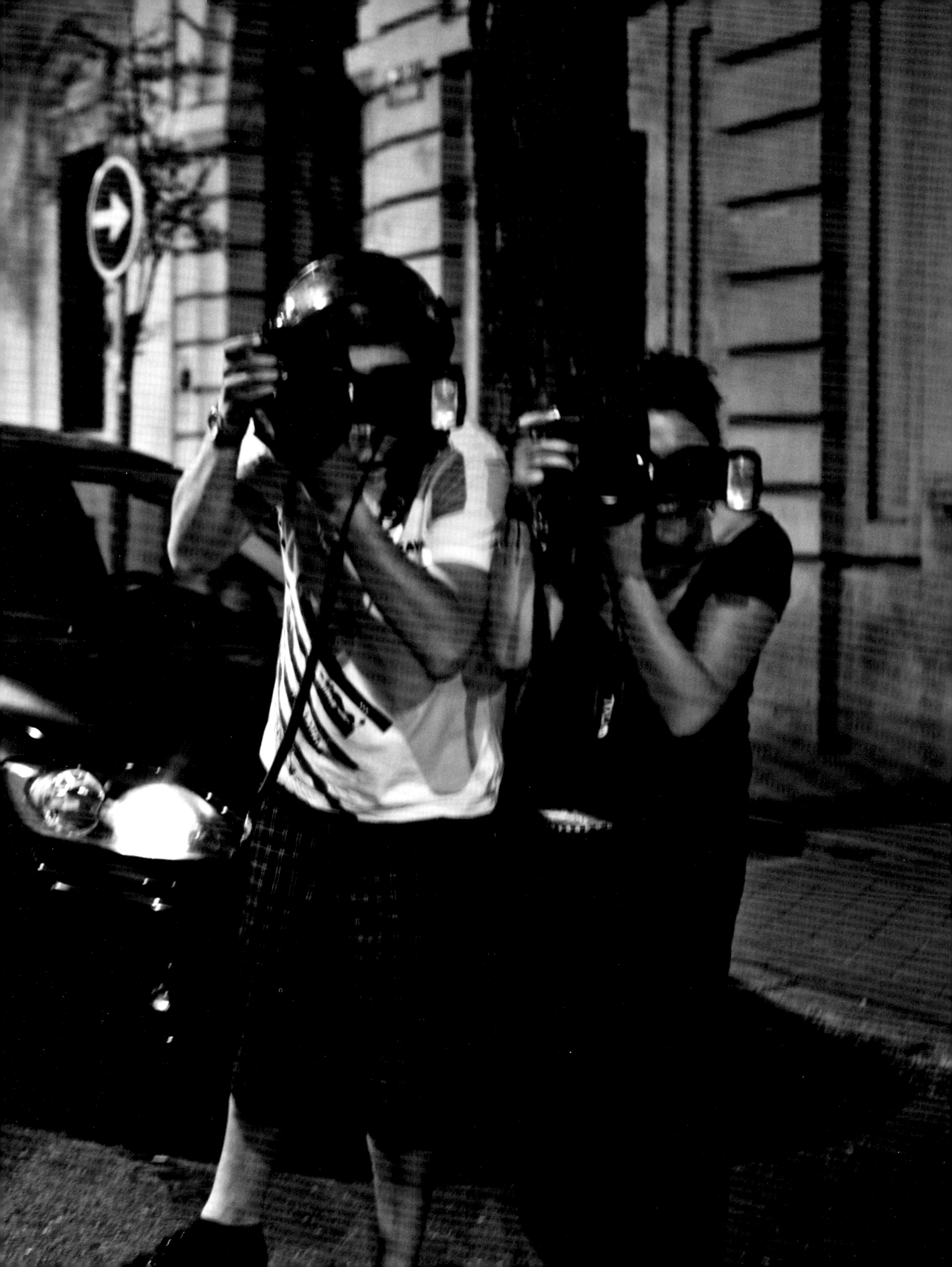

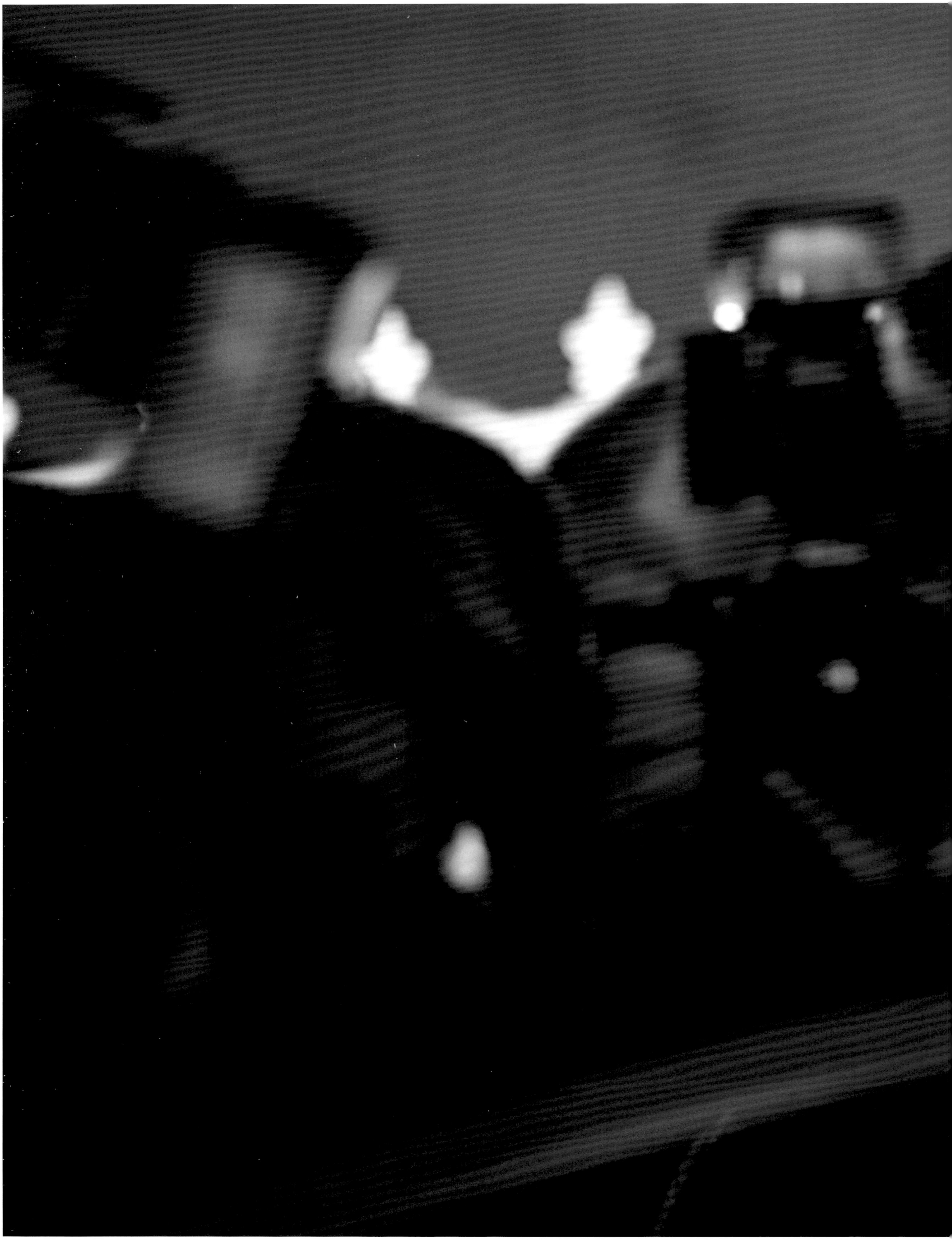

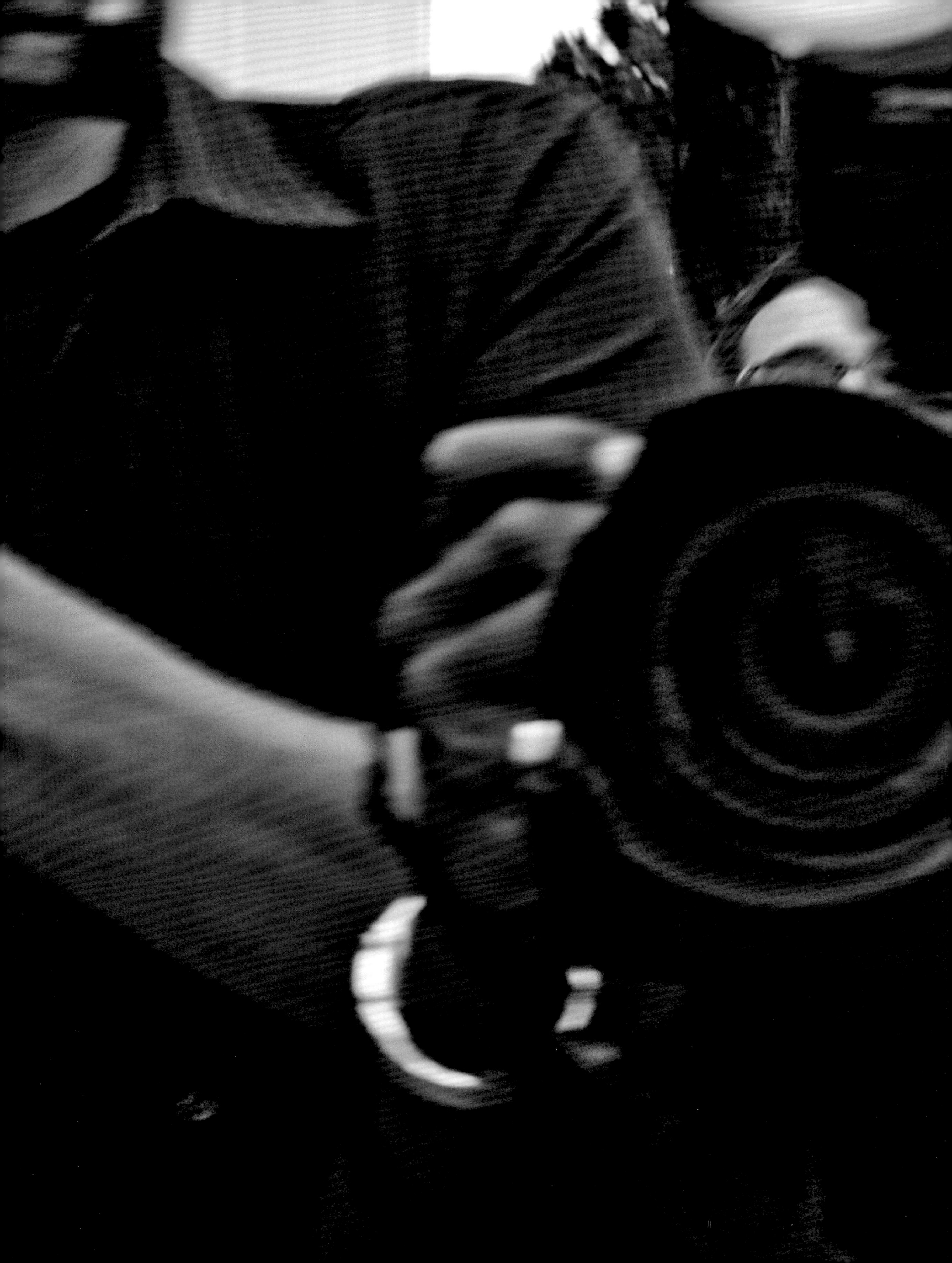

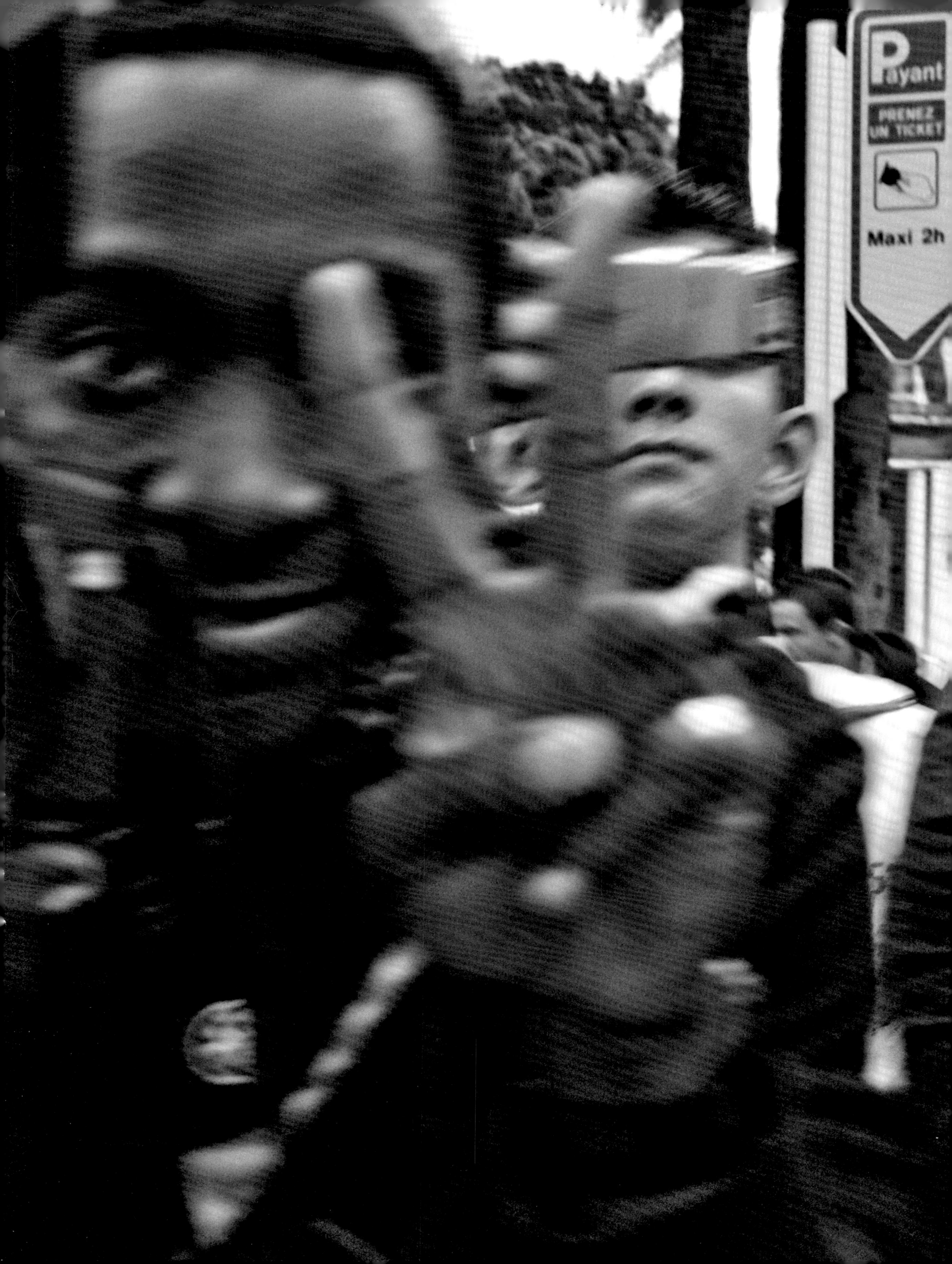
Payant
PRENEZ UN TICKET
Maxi 2h

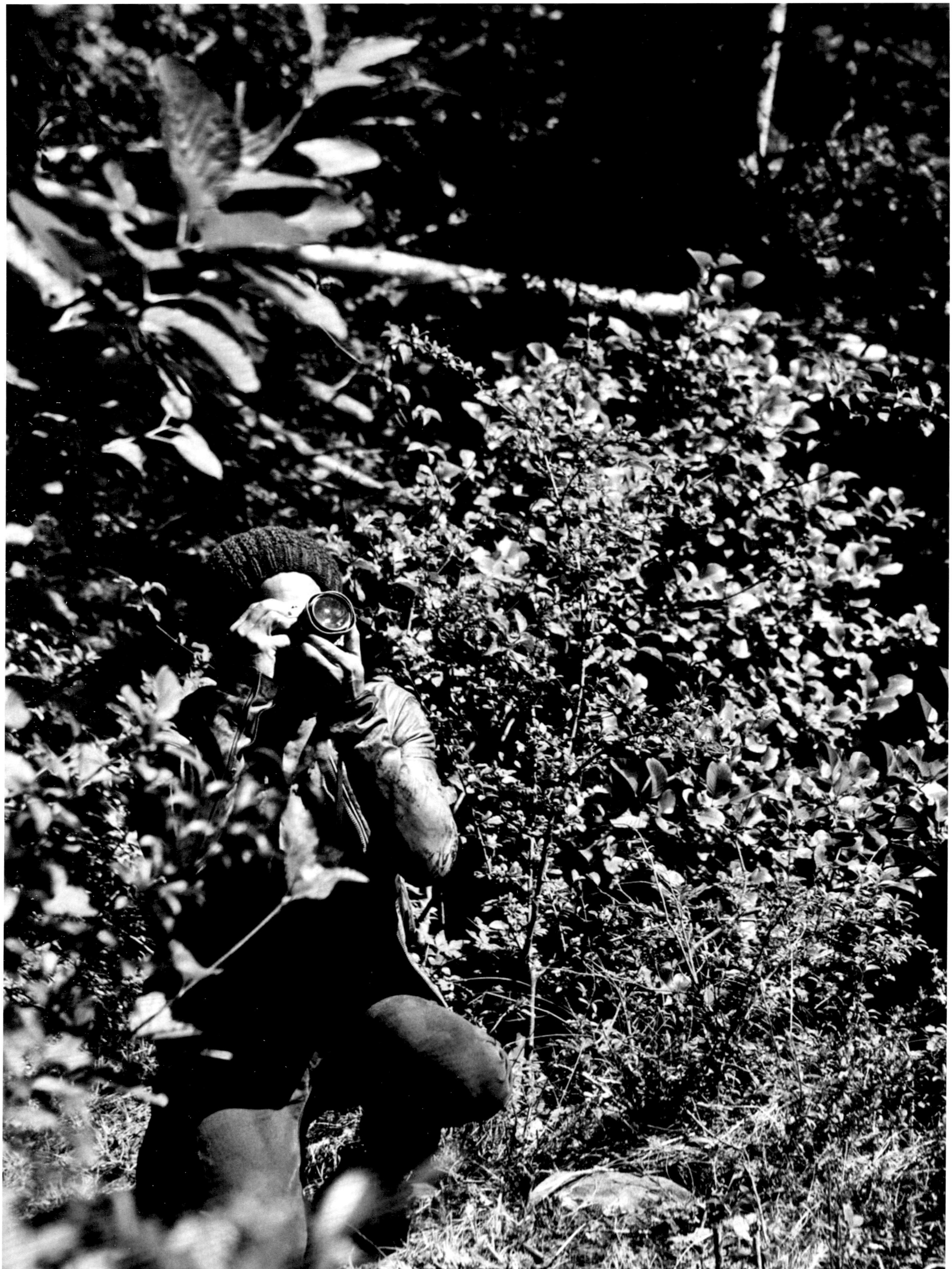

BIOGRAPHY

Regarded as one of the preeminent rock musicians of our time, Lenny Kravitz has transcended genre, style, race, and class into a 25-year musical career—one which revels in the rich influences of '60s and '70s soul, rock, and funk.

Kravitz's talents as a writer, producer, and multi-instrumentalist have resonated through nine studio albums into a timeless catalog. He has won four consecutive GRAMMY Awards, setting a record for the most wins in the "Best Male Rock Vocal Performance" category. Lenny Kravitz's appeal has also been recognized by his peers; his collaborative efforts are as varied as his own influences, having worked with Madonna, Slash, Aerosmith, Jay-Z, N.E.R.D., Mick Jagger, P. Diddy, and Alicia Keys.

Having sold over 38 million albums worldwide, Lenny Kravitz's musical success has afforded him many opportunities to fulfill his creative vision beyond the recording industry. The artist appeared in a supporting role in the critically-acclaimed film *Precious*, and the box office smash film *The Hunger Games*, as Cinna. He reprised this role in the second film, which was released in fall 2013. Lenny was also seen in Lee Daniels' *The Butler* (The Weinstein Company) alongside Forest Whitaker and Oprah Winfrey.

Kravitz launched a creative firm, Kravitz Design Inc., which provides commercial and residential design services as well as specializes in product development and branding. Kravitz Design touts a portfolio of noteworthy ventures, with a range that includes chandeliers for Swarovski Crystal Palace Collection, suites at the SLS Hotel Miami Beach, and Paramount Bay, a 47-story bay front condominium in Miami. Most recently Kravitz Design has undertaken the creative vision for a collection of luxury suites at the SLS Hotel and Casino in Las Vegas as well as L'Arc, a celebrated nightclub in Paris, France. Future projects for Kravitz Design include designs for a nightclub and luxury villa at the Baha Mar Casino and Resort in Nassau, Bahamas set to open this spring. The firm is creating a collection with Rocky Mountain Hardware, renowned for custom-manufactured architectural hardware. Kravitz Design is also collaborating with iconic California lifestyle brand Fred Segal and will be introducing its first-ever designer collaboration called Fred Segal x Kravitz Design.

In 2014, Lenny Kravitz debuted his 10th studio album, *Strut* and embarked on an extensive world tour, performing songs from *Strut* as well as from a distinguished career that has made him one of the most distinctive and successful recording artists of today.

Over a decade ago, already an avid art collector, Kravitz started collecting master photographs ranging from legends such as Diane Arbus and Gordon Parks to Bruce Davidson and James Van Der Zee.

He started collecting cameras as well, feeling a strongest kinship to the Leica brand. Being the subject of thousands of photographs himself, he decided to turn the camera on others, including the paparazzi who have followed him around for a quarter of a century. *FLASH* is the result of this role reversal.

IMPRINT

Introduction by Lenny Kravitz

Conversation with Jean-Baptiste Mondino and
Lenny Kravitz, interviewed by Anthony DeCurtis

Copy editing by Anshana Arora

Art direction & design by Mathieu Bitton
Prepress by Sophie Franke

Editorial management by Nadine Weinhold
Production by Alwine Krebber
Color separation by
ORT Medienverbund, Krefeld, Germany

Artist portrait of Lenny Kravitz

Lenny Kravitz Management:
Craig Fruin & Howard Kaufman

All images have been taken with a Leica camera.
Special thanks to Steffen Keil of Leica Camera AG

MIX
Paper from responsible sources
Papier aus verantwortungsvollen Quellen
FSC® C107556

Published by teNeues Publishing Group

teNeues Media GmbH + Co. KG
Am Selder 37, 47906 Kempen, Germany
Phone: +49 (0)2152 916 0
Fax: +49 (0)2152 916 111
e-mail: books@teneues.com

Press department: Andrea Rehn
Phone: +49 (0)2152 916 202
e-mail: arehn@teneues.com

teNeues Publishing Company
7 West 18th Street, New York, NY 10011, USA
Phone: +1 212 627 9090
Fax: +1 212 627 9511

teNeues Publishing UK Ltd.
12 Ferndene Road, London SE24 0AQ, UK
Phone: +44 (0)20 3542 8997

teNeues France S.A.R.L.
39, rue des Billets, 18250 Henrichemont, France
Phone: +33 (0)2 48 26 93 48
Fax: +33 (0)1 70 72 34 82

www.teneues.com

ISBN: 978-3-8327-3247-9
Library of Congress Control Number: 2014957246

Printed in Italy

Bibliographic information published by the Deutsche Nationalbibliothek. The Deutsche Nationalbibliothek lists this publication in the Deutsche Nationalbibliografie; detailed bibliographic data are available in the Internet at http://dnb.d-nb.de.